Out of Office

SIMON SALT

800 East 96th Street,
Indianapolis, Indiana 46240 USA

Out of Office

Cover photographs by Yuri Arcurs and Ronstik/Shutter Stock

ISBN-10: 0-7897-5092-9
ISBN-13: 978-0-7897-5092-1

Library of Congress Control Number: 2013952805

Printed in the United States of America

First Printing: March 2014

Trademarks

All terms mentioned in this book that are known to be trademarks or service marks have been appropriately capitalized. Que Publishing cannot attest to the accuracy of this information. Use of a term in this book should not be regarded as affecting the validity of any trademark or service mark.

Warning and Disclaimer

Every effort has been made to make this book as complete and as accurate as possible, but no warranty or fitness is implied. The information provided is on an "as is" basis. The author and the publisher shall have neither liability nor responsibility to any person or entity with respect to any loss or damages arising from the information contained in this book.

Special Sales

For information about buying this title in bulk quantities, or for special sales opportunities (which may include electronic versions; custom cover designs; and content particular to your business, training goals, marketing focus, or branding interests), please contact our corporate sales department at corpsales@pearsoned.com or (800) 382-3419.

For government sales inquiries, please contact governmentsales@pearsoned.com.

For questions about sales outside the U.S., please contact international@pearsoned.com.

Editor-in-Chief
Greg Wiegand

Sr. Acquisitions Editor
Katherine Bull

Development Editor
Amber Avines

Managing Editor
Kristy Hart

Project Editor
Andy Beaster

Copy Editor
Bart Reed

Indexer
Tim Wright

Proofreader
Sarah Kearns

Publishing Coordinator
Kristen Watterson

Cover Designer
Chuti Prasertsith

Compositor
Nonie Ratcliff

CONTENTS AT A GLANCE

TABLE OF CONTENTS

About the Author

Photographer, author, writer, and speaker **Simon Salt** has been working from locations that are definitely Out of Office for more than six years. He has been quoted by the *Wall Street Journal, Forbes*, and various other print and online publications and has spoken to audiences across the globe. He presents topics as diverse as mobile, digital, and social marketing and creativity. He also has a comedic session on how to speak English the English way.

Educated in Britain, Simon has degrees in Information Technology, Business and Finance, and Behavioral Science. He also has a master's degree in Logic, Text, and Information Technology—but he still has yet to pass high school math! He is a lifelong learner and is currently attempting to learn Spanish.

Simon is a strong believer in community service and has served as a volunteer firefighter, led a wildland search-and-rescue team, is a certified FEMA Community Emergency Response Team trainer, and currently rides with the Patriot Guard Riders honoring fallen service personnel.

This is Simon's third book, and is already planning his next one—he is also considering therapy to help his addiction to writing. When not sitting at a keyboard, Simon is behind a camera, helping tell other people's stories—something he loves to do.

Dedication

This book is dedicated to the four women who have inspired and continue to inspire me the most:

Alicia Helen Salt, my mother, who inspired an early love of words (in memoriam).

Gemima Salt, a wonderful daughter who has grown into the most amazing woman.

Tessa Salt, so full of talent—a daughter to make any father proud.

Michelle Lemire, my life partner and so much more, and without whom I would not be growing, evolving, and becoming the type of man I'd like to be friends with.

Acknowledgments

Any author will tell you that although their name might be the only one on the cover, no one writes a book alone. I am indebted to the people who have helped me with this book in more ways than they know:

- Katherine Bull, my long-suffering acquisitions editor and friend.
- Amber Avines, for keeping my English more grammatically correct than I ever would.
- Jennifer Pariseau, psychologist, family therapist, and most importantly a long-time friend. We met as students and were reunited via Facebook. I am extremely privileged to have had Jennifer help me with this project. If you are looking for a great family therapist in the Seattle area, talk to Jennifer (http://thenurturedparent.com/).
- Ilene Haddad, an insanely talented individual with whom it has been a pleasure to work on several projects in the past. I was so glad when Ilene agreed to collaborate with me on this project. I think her chapter illustrations bring a little levity to the book. You can see more of her illustrations at http://www.casaweenie.com/.
- There is one other person who, for reasons far too complicated, cannot be named here but knows who they are. Without your help, comments, and friendship, there would be no book with my name on it.

Thank you to this cool team of people.

A book that only shared my thoughts might be a little on the dry side. By using the service Help A Reporter Out (HARO; www.helpareporter.com), I was able to connect to a lot of wonderful individuals who were willing to share their stories with me. I am very grateful to everyone who took the time to respond. I am especially thankful to the following people who shared stories and thoughts with me that I was able to incorporate into the book:

Kevin Ohashi, Jimmy Martin, Wes Rogers, Pavel Mikoloski, Adam Itkoff, Pam Consear, Jamie Pritchser, Kirsten Westberg, Steph Calvert, Denise Snow, Edward Carroll, Shelley Hunter Kukuk, Kathryn Vercillo, Katie McCaskey, Thursday Bram, Faith Amon, Ruksanah Hussein, Jeff Zbar, Haralee Weintraub, John Miller, Eric Nagel, Shel Horowitz, Dayna Steele, Dan Ramirez, Arthur Cooper, Jacque Miller, Robert Pearce, Carolyn Pearson, Donna Ledbetter, Steven MacDonald, Lidia Varesco Racoma, Adrienne Capollupo, Kim Miller, and Sheila Kale

We Want to Hear from You!

As the reader of this book, *you* are our most important critic and commentator. We value your opinion and want to know what we're doing right, what we could do better, what areas you'd like to see us publish in, and any other words of wisdom you're willing to pass our way.

We welcome your comments. You can email or write to let us know what you did or didn't like about this book—as well as what we can do to make our books better.

Please note that we cannot help you with technical problems related to the topic of this book.

When you write, please be sure to include this book's title and author as well as your name and email address. We will carefully review your comments and share them with the author and editors who worked on the book.

Email: feedback@quepublishing.com

Mail: Que Publishing
ATTN: Reader Feedback
800 East 96th Street
Indianapolis, IN 46240 USA

Reader Services

Visit our website and register this book at quepublishing.com/register for convenient access to any updates, downloads, or errata that might be available for this book.

Introduction

If you don't like change, you're going to like irrelevance even less.

—General Eric Shinseki

With the changing nature of office work as we understand it, I felt it was time to create a book for those who are considering or have already made the move to a nontraditional work space. This might be a coffee shop, a co-working space, or even the beach. I use the umbrella term "Out of Office" throughout the book to encompass these nontraditional spaces and the process of working in them.

In this book, I will be using several terms that apply to the different forms of Out of Office working. I define them in the following way:

Work at home—These are individuals who are working for themselves. They are also referred to as *solopreneurs*. Although these solo workers are primarily based at home, they may also utilize some of the same locations as others following the Out of Office work style, such as coffee shops, co-working spaces, and so on.

Telecommuter—This individual works remotely from a home-based office for an organization. They share many of the same challenges as the work-at-home individual but have the additional challenges of being part of a larger organization and managing that dynamic.

Workshifter—This is an individual who spends the bulk of their time away from the organization's offices, but not necessarily at their own home. They make the greatest use of nontraditional work locations such as airports, hotels, coffee shops, co-working spaces, and anywhere they can get an Internet connection, including their car.

Where a section of the book refers to a specific style of Out of Office worker, or at least has more applicability to that work style, I have indicated as much with one of the icons used here.

Who Works Out of Office?

The type of work conducted by these individuals has a common core to it. It is primarily focused around the manipulation of data and information. This leads to them being referred to as *information* or *knowledge workers*—a phrase coined by Peter Drucker in 1959 to highlight that the work product of these types of employees is knowledge rather than a traditional tangible output. The types of jobs this encompasses has increased manifold since Peter Drucker coined the term. From lawyers and accountants, which Peter Drucker would have been familiar with, to those who operate online businesses, provide customer service for large organizations, and fulfill various types of marketing roles. As the types of roles have changed, businesses are finding it necessary to change and evolve the nature of what constitutes an office space.

There are many types of workers who do not work in a traditional office and have no need to—mechanics, delivery drivers, and so on. These workers are not included in the scope of this book.

What's in the Book?

This book contains the result of collecting stories, information, and guidance for people who are considering working from a nontraditional space, either on their own or as part of a larger organization, and for those who are already doing so but want to do it more successfully.

The book is organized in the following way:

- **Chapter 1: Why You Shouldn't Try an Out of Office Experience**

  This chapter lays out why working in a nontraditional setting might not be the best choice for you. It includes a self-assessment test as a guide to deciding whether this style of working is for you.

- **Chapter 2: The Benefits**

  This chapter explains the ways that working Out of Office can be beneficial to your productivity, to your organization, and to your personal life. It includes contributions from people who are already embracing this type of work style successfully.

- **Chapter 3: The Challenges**

  This chapter provides a look at the challenges faced by those who do not work in a traditional office setting—from ensuring you have enough space in your home, to dealing with the noisy coffee shop or the lack of Wi-Fi in your hotel.

- **Chapter 4: Working from Home**

  This chapter shows how people can and do create effective work spaces in their homes. It covers the things to consider when setting up a work space in your home and how to set boundaries in both the physical and relationship sense to ensure you stay productive and that your personal life doesn't suffer.

- **Chapter 5: Working on the Road**

  This chapter tackles the challenges presented by working in remote locations, from airports and hotels to airplanes and trains. It also covers the tools that make it easier, the technologies that make it more efficient, and some of the security concerns you need to be aware of.

- **Chapter 6: Getting Organized**

  This chapter explains how those working Out of Office for larger organizations can be integrated with co-workers in a traditional office setting. It also explains how to effectively set working hours that take into account your own needs as well as the needs of clients, partners, and family.

- **Chapter 7: Rule Setting**

  This chapter details how to avoid working 24 hours a day, seven days a week. You'll learn how to say no to others and still be productive as well as how to set rules but still retain flexibility.

- **Chapter 8: Work/Life Integration**

  This chapter explains why trying to achieve "balance" isn't working and how to achieve a better state of integration. It details the measures to put in place so you can take time off from your business and not have it collapse. It also explains how being Out of Office doesn't have to mean you are "out of mind" with co-workers.

- **Chapter 9: Time to Go Back to the Office**

  Is it time for you to go back to the traditional office setting? This chapter covers how to tell and how to make the transition. Is it time to grow your business and hire others? This chapter explains how to work with remote teams that are helping build your business.

- **Chapter 10: Tools and Tech to Help**

  The final chapter in the book presents a collection of handy tools and technology I use or that have been recommended to me by others.

Whether you're considering the move to an Out of Office work style for yourself or for your employees, this book aims to guide you through the pitfalls, highlight the advantages, and arm you with the information necessary to make an informed decision.

There are definitely challenges to be faced, but there are also many benefits to this new style of working—for both the individual and the organization. Just as society as a whole is evolving and embracing new norms, so is the workplace. Working Out of Office is the next step in the evolution of the office environment.

Where This Book Was Written

I thought it might be fun to share where this book was written, given that I am an Out of Office worker:

- Sixty five percent of the book was written from my home office, which I confess also means the couch in the living room, the balcony, and occasionally from bed.

- Fifteen percent of the book was written in airports, on planes, and in hotel rooms.

- Ten percent of the book was written in coffee shops; this includes those I visited while traveling as well as ones local to me. So, parts of this book have been written in the UK, Italy, and Hong Kong as well as various states within the U.S.

- Five percent was written at conferences during those moments when I had a conversation with someone about the book's topic and they shared an insight or gave me an idea, and I just knew that I had to write it down. Typically this is where my notebook and pen come in handy.

- Five percent was written while doing other tasks, such as shopping, traveling in the car, or sightseeing. I use voice notes for this type of writing and transcribe them later.

Wherever you find yourself working Out of Office, I hope you are enjoying it as much as I do.

Simon Salt, 2014

Why You Shouldn't Try an Out of Office Experience

At the end of a short hallway, just past the guest bathroom, in our two-bedroom apartment is what the floor plan shows to be a second bedroom. It is a large-ish room that's on the interior of the apartment so it has no external windows. It has a large closet in it and a connecting door to the guest bathroom.

It isn't a bedroom, though; it is my office. The walls are decorated with a whiteboard, a corkboard (covered with things that remind me of places I've been), a hook with numerous speaker badges on lanyards hanging from it, and a framed article (the first magazine article I had published). Also, two firefighter helmets (from my time as a volunteer firefighter) hang above the closet door.

My desk, which formerly occupied the office of a lawyer, is large, with a leather top and numerous drawers. It dominates one wall. The other free space is taken up by a futon (the guest bed).

This is my space. Yes, it is a guest bedroom, and I am evicted when we have guests stay over—but for the most part, it is mine. I can shut the door when I am on a call or leave it open as I please.

I can play my music or watch YouTube videos as loud as I want. It is a fortress of solitude in many ways. It is also part of my home. A home I share with my partner and pets.

The dream of escaping the 8-to-6 grind, the cubicle, and the endless meetings can seem like a utopia. Working "Out of Office" isn't for everyone, though. Some of those people who do perform the "escape" end up just as unhappy as they were before. Therefore, before you leap, let's take a look at why you might *not* want the Out of Office experience.

I've been working Out of Office for more than six years. I have had many discussions about how easy (or not) it is with others who also use this work style as well as with those who are working from the more traditional in-office setting.

WHAT IS AN OUT OF OFFICE WORKER?

For the purposes of this book, I am focusing on knowledge/information workers. Of course there are many who do not work from an office. However, I focus on those who would traditionally have found themselves working in an office but because of changes in technology and attitudes are now enabled to work from other locations.

- **Solopreneur**—This is the solo worker, working for themselves. This person works primarily from home but also utilizes some of the same locations as workshifters and telecommuters, such as coffee shops and co-working spaces.

- **Telecommuter**—This person works for an organization remotely, usually from home, and shares much of the same challenges as the solopreneur. However, the telecommuter has the additional challenges of being part of a larger organization and managing that dynamic.

- **Workshifter**—This person has been called the "Road Warrior" in the past. This is an individual who spends the bulk of their time away from the organization's offices, but not necessarily at their own home. They make the greatest use of nontraditional work locations, such as airports, hotels, coffee shops, co-working spaces, and anywhere they can get an Internet connection, including their car. Some of my time working Out of Office has been as part of larger teams, some of which were not only separated from me by distance but culture—even based in different countries. I've also been running my own based-from-home business for five years while working with clients from around the world as well as having freelancers based around the United States.

Some people are self-aware enough to know in advance that they just don't have the right personality type to work from home or in nontraditional settings.

Others are unsure if they have what it takes; they are unsure what is involved in this type of work style as well as what the advantages and disadvantages are. My hope is that this chapter will help these people gain some insight into the drawbacks and challenges faced by those who have chosen or have been directed to work "Out of Office."

Although many people dream of having a flexible work life, coming and going as they please, and not facing the gloomy vista of a cubicle wall day in and day out, for most the Out of Office experience is little more than that—a dream. Some roles just can't be completed effectively away from the traditional in-office setting, and for some people the distractions, the lack of structure, and the lack of social context is just too overwhelming to allow them to be effective.

To assist you in deciding whether you might be suited to the Out of Office work style, I've worked with a professional therapist to create a self-assessment quiz. The quiz can be found at the end of this chapter, and is also available online at www.outofofficesuccess.com. Although created by a professional, the quiz is meant as a guide, not as a professional assessment of your abilities, personality, or personal traits. So please don't base life-changing decisions solely on the quiz. It will, however, give you some ideas about whether the Out of Office work style is something you could explore, either as an individual or within the larger setting of your corporate employment.

But before we start looking at the self-assessment, let's discuss a few of the reasons why, in general terms, you might want to think twice about making the leap from the In Office environment to the Out of Office environment.

You Are Too Social

Although your colleague in the next cubicle might annoy you on a daily basis, regaling you with stories of how their new baby is so cute or how their puppy did at obedience classes, or driving you crazy with the sound of fingernails being clipped, they are part of the social fabric that makes up your daily life.

Remove them, and part of your daily life is removed as well. Now on the face of it you might think it would be a relief to have this person gone, but as human beings we have evolved to be social—even if we have annoying work colleagues. Yes, they get on your nerves, and, sure, the first conversation you have when you get home and talk to your partner is about how annoying your work colleagues were that day, but (and it is a big but) they give you a frame of reference for your work. You know they will be there each day, you know they will annoy you, but you also know that those sounds that come from the next cubicle over are signs of life.

On the other hand, you may work in a place where you love your fellow co-workers, where work life and family life blend in a way others can only dream of. You and your colleagues work hard together, play hard together, have each other's backs, and enjoy each other's company. Maybe you play in a softball league together or enjoy Sunday football in each other's homes. Perhaps your children are friends with each other.

Now imagine you are at that social gathering, watching football on a Sunday, but suddenly you have no point of reference for the conversations about office activity. You weren't there when a certain joke was told, you weren't in that amazing presentation, and you weren't present when the new client signed the big deal.

No matter how close you were to those people, you are going to feel like an outsider, because if you are no longer part of the everyday life of the office, that is exactly what you are—an outsider. The support network that people establish through being in the same place and sharing experiences with the same group of people on a daily basis—sometimes for years on end—cannot be underestimated. It is a factor in the reason behind some people never changing jobs; they find a place where they are comfortable and they stay for as long as they can.

Here is a tale of one person who tried the Out of Office work style and found that they missed the interaction too much to continue:

> *I find that my people interaction needs are too high and not satisfied with electronic interaction only. The irony, of course, is I spent countless hours on conference calls and in front of my PC at the office. But being with smart, diverse people every day is more stimulating than with them on the phone or PC. So I do a lot of nonprofit work to ensure I am getting that stimulation that only comes when you are seeing a smile or looking someone in the eye. **Heck, I like dealing with conflict and anger better face-to-face.***

I love the last line in this story (the emphasis is mine); it was something I hadn't even considered, but it is very true. Conflict and anger are much better resolved when the people concerned can actually see each other, can see their opponent(s), and can use not only verbal but nonverbal communication as part of the resolution.

Although popular culture would have us believe that people are in fact changing careers all the time, this is really a myth—a myth often given credence by pundits vaguely citing the Bureau of Labor Statistics (BLS). So bad has this myth become that the BLS issued a memo in March 2012 stating that "no consensus has emerged on what constitutes a career change."

In fact, it seems that once employees find a place where they like the work and the people around them, they tend to stay. Although many people would like to say that they love the job they do, many simply do it to pay the bills. So if it isn't the work, what keeps us in one place? The obvious answer has to be the people. Of course, income security, benefits, location, and lack of alternatives play a strong role in maintaining a position as well. However, given that work life is at least eight hours a day, five days a week, the people we share a work space with are the primary social group in most of our lives.

For those people who find themselves hanging out with their colleagues after work and on the weekends, and even taking vacations with them, a work life centered around just themselves rather than a team might not work out so well.

The concept of the eight-hour day is, in reality, less of a truism and more of a vague wish by senior managers. It would be a rare individual who arrives at the office, sits at their desk, and in a constant uninterrupted stream works for eight straight hours without a break. Leaving aside breaks for biological needs, if you factor in a 30-minute lunch break and twice-a-day refreshment (or smoke) breaks of ten minutes, you have already reduced the working day by nearly an hour.

That would be the most effective worker on their most effective day. Yes, I know people eat at their desks and continue to work, but I would argue that they are not working at 100-percent effectiveness, even if they are still operating a keyboard one handed while consuming a sandwich.

Now let's take a more realistic look at a worker's day: Few information workers work alone; they are reliant on others within the organization who are up and down stream of them in the flow of information. Their work is dependent on the constant flow of that information, in much the same way production line workers are dependent on the stations before them in the line, providing the parts needed for their role. When that flow is interrupted or the information needs clarification, then the bane of the organizations occurs—the dreaded meeting.

 Note

For the purposes of this book, I am defining an information work or knowledge worker as a person whose primary output of production is information or knowledge, as opposed to those workers who produce tangible products. Lawyers, marketers, public relations, software developers, writers, and so on would all fall into this definition.

Sometimes a meeting is just a gathering at someone's cube, and sometimes it's something more formal. Although meetings might be painful to attend, according to popular culture, they in fact often provide a needed break from the routine and a chance to catch up with co-workers, whether about work-related matters or social ones (usually they provide an opportunity for both).

Here is a story from someone who tried the Out of Office work style but decided it just wasn't for them:

> *It is fully possible to perform my duties from home on my personal computer. When I was hired I thought I would give it a try, working from home. However, it only lasted about a month and I had to go into the office in Seattle.*
>
> *Living, sleeping, and working all within the same space was not a good idea for me. All throughout college I had tried my best to separate school and home life. I would stay up late on Monday through Thursday writing papers, doing research and homework so that I could go home on the weekends and not have to do anything for school. I would refuse to do homework at home.*
>
> *I wanted to have the separation between "work" and home life. I was able to manage that schedule for four years. I don't know why I thought it would be different this time.*
>
> ***Probably the most important reason I moved back to the office was to have face-to-face interaction and to get out of the house.*** *I found that during the month I worked from home the only time I left the house was to visit my parents or to meet up with friends. I needed a change of scenery and a change of pace.*
>
> *I now work in the office in Seattle, which is much better. I have to look sharp for work, and I get to have my much-needed human interaction.* ***Moving back to the office, easily one of the best decisions I ever made. Period.***

That's a pretty telling story. The emphasis is mine, but clearly for this individual working from home was *not* something they could adjust to.

The need for face-to-face interaction was just too great, and they recognized that about themselves and rejoined their colleagues in the more traditional in-office setting, which they felt was the best decision they could have made.

This face-to-face time is very necessary for the social-oriented worker. As we know, a significant percentage of human communication is conducted nonverbally (not the often misquoted 93 percent, but still a significant amount). Therefore, when we have physical meetings and are able to see the speakers' faces, we are able to gather other cues to help us understand their message in its entirety.

This is also part of the social need for many people to work with others—the need to pick up on nonverbal cues as indicators of the true nature of an interaction. How many times have I wished for a "sarcasm" font when writing a document, email, or blog post? Some forms of communication benefit from the nonverbal cues that accompany them, and some fail completely without these cues.

For the social-focused worker, the companionship provided by being part of a traditional in-office environment gives them the "social fix" they don't always receive outside of the office. Never is this more true than for those who live alone, for those who have recently migrated to a new part of the country, and for those who do not have a support circle developed outside of the workplace. For these people, spending their working days alone or having limited exposure to other people (and especially other colleagues) would be a draining experience and one that would ultimately impact their ability to be effective workers. Therefore, not only do they lose out, but so does their employer.

This is definitely something anyone considering the move to an Out of Office work style should consider: How do they handle long periods of time in their own company. Later in the book we'll look at coping strategies, but if this fundamental requirement (being able to go for prolonged periods without social interaction) is not something that a person can adequately cope with, it is fairly certain that the nonconventional Out of Office work style will not be a good fit for them as a permanent move—although that isn't to say it couldn't be handled as an interim measure.

So if you are the life and soul of the office and the go-to person when anyone in the office needs something, working outside of the traditional office environment might not be the best move for you. If you look forward to Monday morning and getting back to the noise and hustle of the office environment, then the Out of Office life style is probably going to be a disappointment.

Of course, working Out of Office doesn't mean working in isolation; it's not solitary confinement. There are varying lengths of time, for different roles, that will mean working alone or working around strangers. Although working around strangers can actually be invigorating for some, it can be a major distraction for others. Especially if you are particularly social, the opportunity to meet new people can be a great attraction to working Out of Office, but it doesn't necessarily aid productivity.

I've been working out of the traditional office environment for six years now, and there have been times while I have been writing that I will suddenly realize that, with the exception of my girlfriend, I have not seen another living soul for four or five days. Some people will say that isn't healthy, and although I'd agree that prolonged isolation is not good for you, some people just have personalities that suit being away from the madding crowd better than others—and I happen to believe I'm one of them.

You Are Too Easily Distracted

Working Out of Office is a great, almost endless, source of distractions. Working from home means that you are subject to all the domestic distractions that home life brings. After all, you are home all day, so would it really hurt you to do the laundry, walk the dog, get the groceries, run a few errands, pick up the kids from school? The list, like the distractions, is endless.

Then of course there is TV, the Internet, books, magazines, hobbies, and a dozen other things that can be done instead of work—all of this just in your own home. Why not use the gym when no one else is there, perhaps in the middle of the day? That way, you'll get a great workout in and not have to wait on the machines.

Surprisingly, although we think of technology as the great distractor, there are several technological solutions that enable you to shut out distractions created by technology. Of course, the simplest and easiest to use is the on/off button. Turn your phone off and it can't distract you! Also, software is available that will put certain websites on a timer. For example, if you are working on a presentation and you really don't need the distraction that Facebook provides, you can set the software to block Facebook for a given period of time. For some, music is a distraction, but for many others it can aid concentration. Certainly some studies seem to support that view, and listening to music through earphones is a great way to block out the noise from a coffee shop or public transport. There are mental exercises you can undertake to help you increase your ability to focus on tasks. Although we all love to think of ourselves as amazing multitaskers, the reality is we aren't. If you are finding yourself becoming easily distracted, one solution, if you have the time, is to give into it. Being distracted could well be a sign that you need to take a break from the current task, so do it, but in a controlled way that doesn't mean you miss a deadline.

For the easily distracted, working Out of Office can be like letting a child loose in a candy store—there are so many things to catch the eye, so many new things to be tried, so many other things than work to capture the mind. Although there's actually no reason why work has to be organized around a traditional schedule of 8 a.m. to 5 p.m., Monday to Friday, there does have to be some organization, especially when the person working Out of Office is actually part of a larger team, some of whom are working in a traditional setting.

Escaping the home and working from an alternate location might be a solution for some, but sometimes this just increases the distractions. Coffee shops, airports, train stations, bookstores, and so on are all great places to work. Many provide power, Wi-Fi, even food and drink to keep you going, but they are also great places for people watching—and what greater distraction can there be for a human being than to sit and watch other humans going about their lives? We are all voyeurs, and social technologies have only increased this habit in many people. How many people's Facebook walls did you "browse" today?

A coffee shop can be like a Facebook wall in real life. People get lost in their own worlds; you get to listen in on phone calls, see what people are reading, what websites they are surfing, and of course what their favorite beverage is.

Airports are just as rich an environment. I have seen some amazing outfits being worn in airports and had to scratch my head in wonder as to why someone would wear something like that on a plane (never mind wear something like that in public). There are the stories of reunions, of meetings and goodbyes, all to be witnessed. In fact, if you are in an airport long enough, you will see all of the human emotions expressed. You'll witness anger, love, laughter, tears, hellos and goodbyes, and the wonder on children's faces as they press them against the big glass windows and watch planes come and go.

Hotel lobbies are rich environments, too, with people checking in, checking out, and passing through. Who are all these people? What are their stories? Are they on vacation, business, meeting an illicit lover?

How can you not be distracted by all that humanity?

Of course, you are also part of that social tapestry that others are watching, not some removed observer; your actions can invite interaction from those around you. Another distraction! There is always someone who wants to start up a conversation. I'm a very antisocial traveler on planes, I put my earphones in before we have taken off—hopefully a clear sign to fellow travelers that I have no intention of joining in a conversation. But some people just love to chat on planes, and all those good intentions you had of getting a couple of hours work done on the flight just went out of the window as you get sucked into a long conversation about whatever topic is most pressing to that person at the moment.

I'm not suggesting that you have to become insular and reject the humanity around you, but knowing that those around you can be a constant source of distraction and recognizing how susceptible you are to it is an important factor in understanding how well you are going to cope with the Out of Office work environment.

Can you tune out those distractions, or are you like the dog in the movie *Up*, constantly pulled one way and another by squirrels? If squirrels (and by that I mean distractions) are your thing and you have an issue tuning them out, then working in a place filled with them is probably not the best move for you if you want to stay productive. Of course, those places can provide great respite from work and are always great entertainment.

My cell phone is one of my great distractions. I try and remember to put it in silent mode or at least vibrate when I am working, but sometimes I forget. Then the little "ding" noise notifying me I have a new message, email, or Facebook update just lures me away from the keyboard. Even though I know I'm not waiting on anything life changing, I am still a victim to this distraction—you know, just in case there is in fact a life-changing post to Facebook that I would be the last to see!

I work from many different places—primarily my home, but also from coffee shops and all the other places I have mentioned here. So I know just how distracting they can be. I always set out with the best of intentions of getting work done on the road, but inevitably end up either not getting any done or only getting a fraction of what I had imagined completing done. Of course, distractions are really just excuses to avoid doing something we don't want to do, and the cure for that is discipline.

I'll be returning to this theme later in the book and sharing thoughts from a professional therapist about self-discipline, avoidance techniques, and other ways those of us who are easily distracted manage to fool ourselves that it's not really our fault that we are distracted—we are just being social, being helpful, or whatever reason we give ourselves.

From partners to pets, children to errands, the social web to passing strangers, we are all susceptible, to varying degrees, to the distractions that life presents us. How we handle those distractions and how much we let them intrude on our work life is what identifies us as either being suited to the Out of Office work lifestyle or not. Again, this isn't a measure of a person's talent, abilities, or usefulness as an employee.

The ability to tune out distractions is definitely an important facet of a person who is going to work in a nontraditional setting. It can, I believe, be learned, although I think it is one of the more difficult "soft skills" to learn as a worker, especially when working with those who are in a more traditional environment and less open to the same types of distractions.

You Don't Have the Space

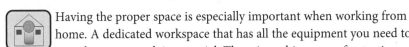 Having the proper space is especially important when working from home. A dedicated workspace that has all the equipment you need to complete your work is essential. There is nothing more frustrating, especially for someone who has been used to the more traditional in-office environment, than to find you can't complete a simple task because you are lacking a tool as basic as a stapler.

But it goes beyond this. As we will look at in Chapter 4, "Working from Home," the space that you work in can directly affect your productivity. Short-term, interim spaces are fine when you just need to rattle off a few emails. That type of work can be done from pretty much anywhere. Heck, I do that sitting on the couch in front of the TV from a laptop. However, can you imagine if your couch were your only workspace? Or perhaps the dining room table, the kitchen counter, or your bed?

This type of thing happened to an Out of Office worker who moved to a smaller place:

> *Working from home did work for a while as long as I had a specific place at home dedicated to work—i.e., created an office. But after I moved, I thought I could do with a smaller place by combining and creating multiuse spaces. It didn't work.* ***I found that working in the office— i.e., having a dedicated space and place—makes me more productive. There are less distractions.***

Again, the emphasis is mine. Although the idea of a multiuse space seems great— and of course less square footage usually means less rent—obviously an opportunity cost is associated with a smaller space. A multiuse space must constantly be reconfigured to suit the activity at the time. Therefore, if your office space is also your dining area, then when you are done working you have to change it back, and when you are finished dining it has to be returned to the work space before you can recommence work. Otherwise, you just become undisciplined and try and work in your dining space or eat in your work space and find, as this person did, that the distractions are just too great.

How productive would you be if these places were your full-time work space? I'd hazard a guess and say not very. We are all more productive when we are comfortable; the right height desk, the right height chair, and so on, all make a difference.

Beyond the physical aspect is the familiarity aspect of a regular work space. Knowing that a particular room is your office and that, when needed, you can shut the door, thereby controlling the space, is incredibly important to most people. In fact, the lack of privacy and inability to shut out distractions is one argument against the cubicle farms that are so pervasive in today's offices.

Knowing where everything is and having it at hand increases our productivity and decreases workplace stress.

So thinking about your workplace and how you will set it up is an important step to take before committing to the Out of Office work style. Is your spare bedroom really going to work as an office? Is the noise from the furnace in the basement going to distract you if you set up down there? Can you afford to make the environmental changes to the property to provide an office space that is both usable and comfortable?

Although these are challenges, working from home at least gives you options regarding the space you use and how you use it. Working Out of Office in public spaces provides much less choice about the space and how it is used. You can rearrange tables and chairs in a coffee shop, but not in a way that inconveniences other patrons, and spreading across a couple of tables with your computer, paperwork, and other items is definitely not going to make you popular.

Other places become even more restrictive. On an airplane, for example, does your computer fit on the drop-down tray? What happens when the person in front of you pushes their seat back and suddenly that small amount of space is reduced even further? Space is an important aspect of our working environment, to the point that most states legislate the amount of space an individual should have as a working environment in commercial properties.

With the best intentions you have of working anywhere, the challenges of doing so can seem insurmountable. One of the major issues of working in a space that you don't own is the lack of control. It can be the smallest of details that provides hurdles. For example, you finally find that spot at the gate in the airport that has a power outlet that isn't being used. You get yourself comfortable, get your laptop plugged in, and start working; you even manage to connect to the free Wi-Fi. Perfect, you are being productive with your wait time. Then you realize that you need a biological break—which means you have to tear down your temporary workspace, pack it up, and head to the restroom, knowing that the chances that the outlet you found will still be vacant are slim at best. The power vultures are already circling, watching you shift in your seat.

I know I am not the only one this has happened to. I've even taken advantage of this happening to other travelers, watching their look of longing and regret as they unplug their devices and pack them up, knowing that I am going to swoop in and set up my own shop as soon as they vacate.

So bad can the power vultures be that I've even found them unplugging me and plugging in their own device; this happened most recently at a conference where I was trying to work during a session. I suddenly noticed the power warning light on my laptop illuminate. I knew I had plugged into an outlet just behind me. I turned around to find that someone had unplugged my cord and plugged in their phone. They looked completely unabashed at me when I asked them to re-plug my cord; they simply shrugged and did it.

The need to control our workspace and the need to remain connected to our alternate world of email, social media, company intranet, and so on, often outweighs our need to be social to those around us. Space is what we want, but we will take whatever we can get and make the most of it if we have to.

HOT DESK

A term derived from the military concept of a hot bed: literally trading a sleeping space with another solider when changing shifts. Hot-desking is less intimate and usually refers to the practice of keeping unassigned workspaces available for field staff when they visit the parent company offices. This practice has now spread to more public spaces such as co-working offices and executive suites.

This approach is hardly ideal, but it is the reality of many who work Out of Office. The front seats of cars, tables on trains, tray tables on planes, and the corner of the bar in a coffee shop—these places serve well for short-term stop gaps, but they lack the space and the familiarity to be permanent arrangements. Enter the hot desk arrangements offered by co-working and by-the-hour executive offices.

Offering the temporary nature of other, more public spaces, these facilities also offer a more private office environment with room to spread. Of course, this convenience comes at a cost not associated with more public, free spaces. But as always, you get what you pay for. The opportunity cost is clear to the Out of Office worker: Lower cost equals less space, and higher cost increases the amount of private space.

Co-working spaces also offer the benefit of having a community/traditional in-office environment, even if the others present aren't exactly co-workers. We'll talk more about the advantages and disadvantages of these spaces in Chapter 5, "Working on the Road."

The space you choose is going to depend on the length of time you are going to need it, the amount of money you want to spend to acquire it, and ultimately how much privacy you need to get your work done. I can't imagine not having my own space at home to call an office; I've always had that even when I worked primarily from a traditional office—a place that I could equally be productive from at home was essential even then. It is more so now that I work full time from home.

Although I am fine working on the road, I find that I am never quite as productive as when I am in my own office. There are many reasons for this, and as highlighted in this chapter, distractions, comfort, and the lack of control of the environment are just a few of them. Sometimes the reasons are practical: The place where I am working lacks Wi-Fi or sufficient power outlets. Sometimes the reasons are more about my focus and whether or not I can discipline myself to work in a strange place.

The familiarity of the place, the ability to walk away from the desk and leave everything as is without packing up and taking it with me, and the knowledge that no matter how obscure the cable, office supply, or device, I have everything within reach just seems to make me more comfortable and therefore more productive.

Whatever space you decide on, it is essential that you ensure you have adequate, comfortable space available to you before you commit to the Out of Office work style. Trying to shoe-horn yourself into an inadequate space after the fact is only going to lead to frustration and an unproductive working environment, which will only increase stress.

One last element to think about when choosing a space is new technology. This means that we are often now connecting back to traditional offices, co-workers, and clients via video. So although you might be comfortable with that collection of teddy bears in your office from your teenage years, or working around a stack of packing boxes that contain who knows what, do you really want them as a backdrop to your video meetings?

Your space, even in your own home, may well be shared (at least in a virtual way) with others. Making it professional and (if only to the extent of the field of view of your camera) tidy, organized, and presentable is another essential forced upon us by modern technology. Yes, you may well be wearing sweatpants under the desk, but more formal work attire on top is going to be needed for an on-camera appearance.

In the same way, your work space shouldn't be distracting to clients, colleagues, and others with whom you are connecting visually. That isn't to say it should be devoid of all personality; just be aware of what is around you, or at least in camera shot. It is not always just the permanent fixtures in your office that can disrupt or distract those who are viewing you.

One of my cats has an uncanny way of knowing when I am doing a video call and will seize that moment to jump into my lap. He has greeted more than one video caller with a close-up of his nose as he inspects the camera—or worse, when he turns tail and decides that they aren't particularly interesting to him.

We'll talk more about the way others in your house can invade your space later in the book. For now, though, when picking a space, especially a permanent one in your home, think through all the needs of the members of your household and how that space impacts them before you start moving the furniture around.

You Need an Office for Clients

Whether we like it or not, sometimes people judge us and our ability to deliver based on their perception of us. Okay, that's a lie—it happens all the time. Whether they base that on the clothes we wear, the number of piercings we have, the color of our hair, or the office we work from, clients and customers judge us by measures we may not be aware of.

For some industries, this is less of an issue. I work mostly from home, as a digital strategist, author, and speaker. My office doesn't matter as much as my ability to get to my clients' offices. If I'm doing a strategy session, I prefer to go to the client, or at least video conference with them so that we are all on the same page at the same time. Also, they tend to relax more in their own surroundings.

Other professions require an office space; for example, would you be comfortable with a lawyer who suggested you meet at your home? Would you be worried that they didn't have an office? Some people would probably be fine with it, but I think many would not be. It's expected that when taking that kind of advice, you receive it in a professional environment, usually the law offices.

Some consultants feel that an office adds an element of professionalism that separates them from "freelancers" and other solo-run businesses that do not have the budget for an office. If this is you, then although I understand, and have even explored those thoughts myself, I would say that you are seeking the more traditional in-office work style and probably will find it harder to adjust to the Out of Office work style.

An office doesn't make you more of a professional; ultimately what gives your business credence is the product you produce or the service you provide. Providing excellence in those areas will overcome pretty much any resistance you might meet from clients or potential clients who want to visit your swanky office.

Of course, if you are chasing those types of people as your source of income, then again perhaps the Out of Office work style isn't going to fit with your overall business plan. It doesn't work for all businesses, nor for all people and certainly not for all target markets. I have clients who are Fortune 500, household names, and they never seem to be bothered that I work from home; rather, they are more concerned that I can deliver a quality service at the right price—and, of course, by reducing my overheads and working from home, I have a competitive edge over other providers who have to support the cost of a large, luxurious office.

Renting an office space is certainly an option for many solopreneurs. It can and in many cases does lead to improved productivity and provides for an alternate workspace that is as (if not more) controllable than a home-based office. This is certainly a factor to consider when looking for viable Out of Office work locations—even though it is technically in an office, it is not the formal organizational setting that I am referring to as "in office."

If the expense of renting an office on your own is something you are unsure about, there are other options.

An office is quite probably the largest expense any individual or organization will take on—whether you rent or purchase, it is a major overhead. Executive offices that rent by the hour or have shorter-term leases are a good solution for this type of situation if you need an office on a frequent basis, but what if your need is more sporadic, less structured? Do you just accept the nature of this type of requirement and pay the overhead, hoping to get utility from a space that you only use infrequently?

Actually, several solutions fit this need. Many co-working spaces provide meeting/conference rooms that can easily be tailored for any meeting and can be rented on an hourly basis.

Their rates are usually lower than those of executive offices, and although they might not present exactly the same image as an executive suit, they are most definitely a step up from a coffee shop table.

Here is a story about an Out of Office worker who chose the co-working space to keep him motivated and sane:

> *I finished graduate school and moved back home to the U.S. in 2010. My plan was to start my own business. I have a background in programming and online marketing and started my first online business at age 16. So this didn't feel unusual. What was unusual was that I was no longer in school. This difference didn't seem like much, but I quickly realized I wasn't being productive after a couple months. Days seemed to disappear.*
>
> **It was hard to get work done with an infinite supply of distractions and no peer group or structure to stop me.** *I was a mess.*

I was lucky enough to recognize it. I tried a lot of different things to spark my productivity. Nothing that kept me at home worked. Four months later I joined Affinity Lab, Washington D.C.'s oldest co-working space. Suddenly, I was in an environment full of other entrepreneurs being productive. It also gave me a social group, which I desperately lacked after moving to a city with very few friends. It got me started and has sustained me for the past 19 months. I built my startup, Review Signal(.com), which I built and launched (last week!) during my tenure at the co-working space. I would have never managed without getting back into an office environment. **I don't need a boss, but I need colleagues for social and professional reasons.** *Having access to 60+ other companies who have faced similar challenges and help each other was the difference between giving up and wasting my time and being productive and launching a product. Getting back into the office environment has kept me sane and even made me happy living in Washington, D.C. again.*

That need for like-minded individuals—to be around those who at the very least share an understanding of what it is like to be facing challenges alone or with only a couple of other people for support—is why co-working spaces are so popular, especially with new entrepreneurs who have yet to build out a team but still need the proximity of others. For employees of larger organizations, co-working spaces can also provide the social setting that they may be missing; however, the infrastructure/security concerns can outweigh the social benefits.

Hotels often have conference rooms as well as meeting rooms that are available for hire for short periods, especially during the week when they aren't being used for conferences or weddings. Although having someone meet you at a hotel might seem awkward, the environment can actually lend itself well to a different kind of professional experience. If you go with a more upmarket hotel, then the furnishing and fittings will certainly be of a higher level than you would find in all except the most formal and expensive of office spaces. Hotels have the advantage over other office spaces of also being able to offer catering services. So if your meeting is going to be timed around lunch, but a restaurant isn't appropriate, why not have lunch catered in the conference room?

Far from being an odd place, the hotel setting can actually enable you to step up your presentation and increase the perceived value of your business, if you think creatively.

Of course, if these elements are outside your budget, or simply don't exist in your locale, then a formal office might be your only resort, and again that is a major consideration to take into account before committing to the Out of Office work style.

You Need Regular Team Contact

The need for regular team contact is a very specific, and although it can apply to almost any profession, I've witnessed it especially among creative people. Part of the creative process is brainstorming, throwing ideas around to see what works.

Working in isolation can lead down some very odd creative paths, and although sometimes those paths can be valuable, they can equally be very poorly thought through. I have no doubt that some of the major missteps that social media has borne witness to in recent years have come from people working in isolation and not having the opportunity to, at the very least, run an idea past a co-worker before hitting the Enter key.

Take, for example, the post on Twitter by Kenneth Cole, CEO of the Kenneth Cole fashion house. He took to Twitter during the early days of the Arab Spring uprisings and posted the following:

> *Millions are in uproar in #Cairo. Rumor is they heard our new spring collection is now available online at http://bit.ly/KCairo -KC*

Now, had he run that past someone, they might—and of course I say *might* because he is the CEO, and who knows whether anyone would tell him otherwise—have pointed out the gauche nature of the tweet and advised against it. Instead, it was posted and caused a huge backlash against Kenneth Cole, both the person and the brand on all its social media properties.

Sometimes even working in a traditional office environment can be isolating, especially if, as a senior executive, you closet yourself from co-workers who might just be more in touch with things than you are. So working in an Out of Office workplace where access to co-workers is even harder to achieve and sometimes may require scheduling appointments presents the opportunity for an even greater chance of these situations arising. One workaround is to simply not enable Out of Office employees to communicate publicly on behalf of the organization. That option is, in my opinion, not only short-sighted, but, in the world in which we now do business, not practical either. Whereas a decade ago corporate communications was limited to strictly those whose role specified that they communicate on behalf of the company, many more employees now find themselves being given the task of utilizing social channels as part of their job and becoming voices for the company. Some of these employees are working Out of Office because of the nature of their role—perhaps they are event organizers, sales support staff, or any one of a number of other roles that are now part of the social teams that have been created in recent years by companies. Silencing these employees not only limits the company but it is detrimental to the development of the individual.

I know many individuals who work in PR, marketing, and corporate communications for large corporates; they work in teams, and before publishing things, whether through social or more formal communication channels, they, at the very least, go through a peer-review process. Sometimes it is formal; other times it is simply a matter of leaning over a cube wall and throwing the idea out there to get a reaction. However, it is done, and getting feedback from team members is an integral part of many jobs, and without regular contact it can be hard to achieve this. Even making use of technology such as phone, email, and video conferencing it isn't always possible to replace the instant nature of being in the same place as your team members—not to mention that without being with them, you can't see what they are working on or whether they have the time to spare to provide the feedback you need. What's more, you can't be used as a sounding board yourself and therefore contribute to the overall team effort.

Working from your home, a coffee shop, or on an airplane, you are denied that peer feedback, or at least denied the instant nature of it, which is sometimes necessary, especially in our now, always-on business environment. Being part of a team is expected from most workers, and those who work in a creative or information-based workplace find this to be especially true. Of course, that is not to say it can't be done, but it takes careful management and usually requires additional time and thought put into the process to ensure it can still be achieved effectively.

This additional time requirement can put an unfair burden on in-office team mates, which can lead to either resentment or the circumnavigating of the Out of Office co-worker. It's important that those in charge and the Out of Office co-worker strive to ensure that this doesn't happen by proving the added value of the team member who works remotely.

Certainly this can be a major reason why an organization doesn't implement Out of Office working, especially for personnel that they consider to be key to a team or process. I'll be discussing the technologies and other methods that can ease this issue, and how some organizations have overcome it, later in the book.

Another of the other issues that can be encountered by Out of Office workers who co-work with those in a more traditional office setting is that as the office culture develops, as shifts occur through either changes in personnel or simply as the team matures, they can miss out on that culture change. They can become trapped in a moment or style of work that the team has moved away from—and suddenly the Out of Office worker seems out of step with the rest of the team. This can be frustrating for both sides. The Out of Office employee feels disconnected with the rest of their team, and the in-office team members view their colleague as being out of touch. This dissonance can lead to a decline in the ability of the team to maintain cohesion, and projects and other work that depends on collaboration can suffer.

Of course, this is an extreme example, and many organizations are more than able to head off this scenario before it becomes a serious problem.

In addition, in many organizations geography within the office environment implies status. If you are allocated to a cube rather than an office, you are probably not as "senior" as those in offices. If your office is on a certain floor, or is perhaps that much vaunted "corner office," you are again more likely to be senior. Although these concepts may seem anachronistic to many, they still persist in the corporate world where the lines of hierarchy that were so clearly delineated a few decades ago have now become increasingly blurred. Where does the Out of Office worker fit into this geography? Perhaps they "hot desk" when visiting the corporate office and work from a spare desk, cube, or meeting room. But what does this imply about their standing within the organization? What does this say to the employees themselves about how the organization views them as part of the internal geography? Although it is often not practical to "reserve" dedicated space for Out of Office individuals, without a place of their own it is easy for Out of Office workers to feel undervalued by the office-based team members.

This confusion can sometimes lead to resistance to ideas, suggestions, and requests from members of staff who are in fact junior to the Out of Office worker but do not realize the role or place the Out of Office worker plays within the organization.

These obstacles can be overcome, but they take work on the part of organizational leaders, HR, and the co-workers involved. Sometimes the resolution is to simply abandon the practice of Out of Office workers or at least reduce the amount of time that a worker spends Out of Office. Although this isn't necessarily the best solution, it is an understandable one—it is the path of least resistance. Certainly organizations have to think carefully before implementing or agreeing to Out of Office working and look to see where the benefits outweigh the burdens that will occur.

Not All Gloom

It isn't all solitude and depression for the Out of Office worker. This would be a very somber and dull book if it was. Throughout the remainder of the book, you will read about many organizations and individuals who make this work style an integral part of the way they work—and do so successfully. The diversity of these organizations, from single-person operations to Fortune 500 companies, is a clear indicator that, when approached properly, the Out of Office work style is a very legitimate way of working.

Like so much else that has been changed by technology, societal shifts, and attitudes to gender roles, work styles are changing, and the pace at which they are changing is accelerating. Although Out of Office working is not yet the norm,

I truly believe we will see an increasing number of people and organizations adopting this work style and realizing the benefits of doing so.

The benefits to both individuals and the organizations they work with and for definitely outweigh the costs. As with any new concept, the early adopters bear the brunt of the cost but also reap the rewards and advantages early.

A good example of a large organization that is supportive of the Out of Office work style is Citrix. They have set up a website at www.workshifting.com as a place where both individuals and organizations can share information about this work style. Of course, Citrix also provides technology that enables Out of Office employees to stay connected to the larger organization, but the fact that they have recognized how much their technology enables it and have actively sought to support the community of Out of Office workers speaks volumes about Citrix as an organization.

This chapter isn't meant to deter you as much as it is meant to assist you with making a decision, having seen some of the realities and challenges that others have faced.

As with many other work styles, working Out of Office can be extremely rewarding and fulfilling, and the flexibility can lead to increases in productivity, loyalty to the organization, and the self-development of the individual working in this way.

Throughout the rest of the book, we are going to look at the other hurdles you will need to overcome to work successfully Out of Office, and I will be sharing more stories from people who have overcome these hurdles successfully.

Out of Office Work Style Self-Assessment

1. Do you enjoy the company social scene?

    a. Very much so, I know everyone's name and family members.

    b. Somewhat so, in order to keep work flowing.

    c. Not much at all. I keep to myself and get my work done.

2. Does your work entail long hours of focus on one major activity?

    a. Not much. I am usually working between writing something up and collaborating with others.

    b. Somewhat. I spend a portion of my day writing up reports, and some of it collaborating with others.

    c. Very much so. I can spend at least a day working on one activity to completion.

3. Are you easily distracted by things around you?

   a. Very easily distracted. I find it difficult to focus if there are other things around me needing my attention.

   b. Somewhat. If it gets too loud or interesting in my work area, I lose focus.

   c. Not much at all. Once I get started on something, I tend to push through to the end.

4. Are you flexible with your time?

   a. No, I need clear boundaries around work time and other life responsibilities.

   b. Somewhat. I need certain work hours designated but can shift that slightly either way.

   c. Yes, I am very flexible and can move things around as needed by work or by other life demands.

5. Do you find it easy to move between tasks if you need to?

   a. No. I become overwhelmed if I am interrupted too often when trying to complete a task.

   b. Somewhat easy. I have times when I am working on tasks that don't demand my full attention and other times when I need to be focused.

   c. Yes, I can easily move between tasks if I need to. Even if it is a task I am focused on, I can handle an emergent issue and then return my focus back to the task at hand.

6. Are you aware of your own reactions to things, people, events as they happen?

   a. No, I don't pay attention to things like that. I just do what I am supposed to do.

   b. Somewhat. I notice when things get really great or really bad.

   c. Yes, I am very aware of how things affect me and how I can use them to change an situation.

7. Are you aware of things that bother you, motivate you, interest you, and bore you?

   a. No, I don't see the point in knowing that much about myself. It's rather selfish, isn't it?

   b. Somewhat. I can tell what bothers me and what interests me

   c. Very much so. I am motivated by _____ and bored by _____.

8. Would your friends and family (and coworkers) say that you are aware of their responses to different things, people and events?

    a. No, I am often hearing that I don't understand or am not paying attention.

    b. Somewhat. My closest family members would say I do.

    c. Yes, very much so. My friends notice how attentive I am to their needs and wishes.

9. Do you love what you do and have a passion for it that sometimes goes beyond your work day?

    a. I do my job and leave it at the office.

    b. Sometimes I find an interesting article or television show related to my work and it grabs my attention.

    c. Very often I find myself seeking out information that relates to my job. I love talking it over with like-minded friends and coworkers.

10. Are your friends and family supportive of you working from home?

    a. They are not aware that I am considering it. I don't think they care either way.

    b. Some of my closer friends and family know that I am considering it and say they are supportive of my efforts.

    c. I have discussed it with family and friends and they are prepared to help me as they can

If you answered mostly A's, then you are probably not the best candidate for working from home as a permanent option. A short period doing this would probably be fine but I wouldn't recommend doing it as a career move.

If you answered mostly B's, then you could probably make this work if you are willing to work on some of the areas that cause you most concern. If not, then you can probably do this for interim periods but shouldn't consider it a full time move.

If you answered mostly C's, then you will love working Out of Office. This is your space and you know how to maximize it to get the most from the opportunity.

2

The Benefits

The benefits to working Out of Office are varied. Many of the benefits are, in fact, real, but many are only imagined by those who have not yet tried the Out of Office work style or have and only fondly remember the parts that worked for them after they have returned to the more traditional in-office work style.

So is it a paradise of sweatpants, favorite coffee shops, working from the patio while watching your dog chase squirrels in the yard?

Actually, yes, or at least for some it is exactly that. I know many individuals who work from home or other locations who seem to spend their days in sweatpants (my personal preference is sleep pants) and who are often found on social networks sharing pictures of themselves (or at least pictures of their feet) in a lounger by the pool—which they lovingly refer to as "the view from their office." Wes Rogers shared this story with me:

> There are times when the most productive thing I can do is step away from the computer. Taking the dog for a walk doesn't work so well in an office, but for me it is a great break for both of us—and I take my iPhone so I'm still available if needed. I've done meetings while walking through the woods or floating in an inner tube in a pool. Unfortunately, the first pool meeting made me a legend because my cell phone and I both fell into the water.

Is it any wonder that those tied to a cubicle look at these pictures or hear these stories and either wish for themselves the same lifestyle or write off the person doing the sharing as someone without a "real" job. After all, who could possibly make a living doing something that can be done from anywhere: To make money, you need a real organization and real teams, departments, budgets, and perhaps most important of all, meetings, lots and lots of meetings. Now that is a real job! Lazing by the pool or working from a coffee shop is only for people who can't get a real job or can only do freelancing work, surely.

Of course, this attitude is borne from jealousy as well as other emotions. The reality is that for many individuals, both those who work for themselves and those who work for larger organizations, the benefits of working Out of Office increase their productivity and make them extremely successful.

However, for every one of those individuals who seem to enjoy a life of leisure, only occasionally seeming to actually be anywhere near anything that resembles "work," I can point you to a dozen others who spend their days running across airport terminals, sitting in endless traffic, or sleeping in anonymous hotel rooms trying to remember what day of the week it is and which city they are in. They are not necessarily living a life of ease; they are hard-working individuals who occasionally get to enjoy some of the benefits of their work style choice. Somewhere in the middle of these two extremes is the majority—those for whom working Out of Office is both a paradise and a necessary evil, both a method of not feeling confined by the traditional in-office work style but also a burden that requires them to work harder to ensure they remain relevant and current to their colleagues.

Remember that much of the paradise is created by the personality of the individual as well as the corporate culture they are operating within. For a solopreneur, the corporate culture is of their making. If they want to work from a formal office setting, they can; equally, if they want to work from a laptop in bed, they are just as free to make that choice. If they decide that they want formal office hours, they can impose them; equally, if they want to work a more flexible schedule, they have the freedom to work in that manner as well.

For those who are tied to a broader, larger corporate culture, the luxuries of sweatpants and a poolside office may seem more like a fantasy than any reality they have encountered. That is not to say there are not benefits for the corporate employees who find themselves working Out of Office; it is just more likely that they will be less of the luxurious type and more of the practical type.

Control of the Environment

One of the big attractions to escaping the more traditional in-office work style is the ability to control the environment in which you work. Of course, the amount of control you have will vary on the location where you choose to work. Public spaces provide a lower degree of control than private ones, obviously. But even these can be controlled to a degree that is sometimes beyond the grasp of the in-office counterpart. For example, if a coffee shop is too loud to work, the Out of Office worker has the choice to put in their earphones and crank up their favorite music tracks to block out the noise; they might even relocate to a quieter setting, which their in-office colleague will find much harder to do.

The Out of Office worker based from home has the highest degree of control over their environment. Want the temperature adjusted? No call to maintenance needed—simply adjust the thermostat. Want to listen to music? Just turn it on—no need to consult with co-workers, or have to listen to *their* music. Want to have a healthy lunch? Simply take it from the fridge—no need to label it with your name and run the risk of someone deciding that it is "share your lunch day" today. The very nature of this work style, which seems isolating and like a stretch in solitary confinement to some, provides freedom and the ability to relax to others.

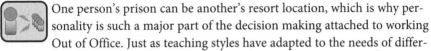 One person's prison can be another's resort location, which is why personality is such a major part of the decision making attached to working Out of Office. Just as teaching styles have adapted to the needs of different learning styles, so too are work styles adapting to the different work-style needs of employees. Just because an individual is not suited to working in an office environment does not mean that they are not able to make a valuable and considerable contribution to an organization. It does, however, require the organization to be willing to release control of the working environment and place that control in the hands of the employee—something that is intrinsically difficult for most organizations, especially the more established, traditional organizations that have decades of employing a particular work style.

Those working Out of Office but not from home still have a considerable degree of control over their environment and how that impacts their productivity. Those who travel a lot get to know their favorite hotels, airport lounges, coffee shops, and other locations that provide them with the perfect mix of noise level, temperature, vista, and other features that encourage productive working while at the same time offer a blend of distractions that provide relief from work. Armed with this knowledge, they are able to navigate their work days with a much greater sense of control than someone who perhaps only travels occasionally. In previous decades, these employees were referred to as "road warriors," mainly because they typically spent their time driving from place to place (and some still do). Work styles have shifted and new methods of selling, such as e-commerce, have replaced the need for many organizations to have field sales teams covering small territories. It is much more likely for a field salesperson to cover several states as a territory now, and they are more likely to do so with a combination of air travel and virtual meetings.

The more time spent working Out of Office, the greater the knowledge of when and where to work grows. These nomads, like their desert-based namesakes, learn to find the best *wadis*. They learn where the outlets are in the airport lounge, which gates have the best coffee shops within two minutes walking distance, which hotel chains have the best Wi-Fi service, and which cities offer the best in public transport. All of these factors are not simply accumulated knowledge; these are the ways in which they get to control their environment.

In the movie *Up in the Air*, George Clooney's character Ryan Bingham shares some of his environmental control knowledge with his protégé:

> *Never get behind old people. Their bodies are littered with hidden metal and they never seem to appreciate just how little time they have left. Bingo, Asians. They pack light, travel efficiently, and they have a thing for slip-on shoes. Gotta love 'em.*

Although part of a fictional exchange in a movie, this type of information is exactly what constitutes the frequent traveler's knowledge of how to control their environment. It is knowledge that has been acquired through experience and allows them to feel a degree of control in an environment that is otherwise rigidly controlled by others. Some might claim that the control is imaginary and based only on an individual's perception. Although that might be true, it doesn't really matter: Perception is reality for most people, and if the Out of Office worker perceives that they have some degree of control over their environment, then for them it is true.

Corporate entities long ago discovered that giving workers the perception that they had a degree of control over their environment benefitted the organization. The Hawthorne experiments of the 1920s and 1930s are often cited as examples of this, and although there is much debate among psychologists over the interpretation of the results and whether the actual change in the environment (that of increasing and decreasing the amount of illumination) had an impact or whether the change of environment to allow for the experiments to take place was the element that caused the change, there is no doubt that a change took place. Therefore, it is important to recognize that for any worker, whether in or out of office, a degree of control of their environment goes a long way to providing them with a feeling of overall control. So perhaps that paradise of sweatpants is less of an illusion than might be thought. It is perhaps more of a statement of control and an expression of the ability to be both productive and comfortable. The Out of Office worker, whether working from home or from other locations, has less of a need to compete with co-workers in terms of personal presentation. With no physical proximity to co-workers, they are less likely to take part in the one-upmanship often seen in a more traditional office setting. They have no cube to dress up and no need to be seen wearing the latest trends or toting the latest gadget.

That is not to say they don't share those interests or even feel driven to be competitive; it is just that by being away from the group, they are less likely to be involved in the "games" of the group.

Beyond comfort, the growing trend for organizations to adopt a "bring your own device" (BYOD) approach to technology is changing the workplace environment by allowing workers to utilize their personal phones, tablets, and laptops and connect them to the corporate information technology infrastructure. I discuss technology and the issues and opportunities it presents in detail in Chapter 6, "Getting Organized." However, this change in attitude allows even those who are in-office workers to control a part of their work environment that was previously completely outside their control. It is also an indication of the increasingly blurring lines between work and personal life. Those who carry a mobile device with them everywhere, regardless of whether it is provided by the organization they are employed by, are now always "on," reachable via email, text message, social network, or voice. What was once a status symbol, and an indication of moving up in an organization, has now become a necessity. Allowing an element of freedom in terms of the choice of device used simply increases the buy-in by the employee to be placed in this role of a 24/7 employee. Technology is, in fact, driving down the hourly wage for the salaried staff member.

As these lines blur, we will see the definition of "workplace" become harder to pin down. Whether or not a person officially works from home, there is no doubt that the expectation that they check email outside of "office hours" is now ingrained in the workforce.

Of course, controlling the environment goes far beyond just the physical elements. One of the biggest features of any large office is the politics—knowing who is in favor, who is not in favor, which person is likely to support your ideas, and who will shoot them down. This is all part of navigating the minefield of the corporate environment. As Pavel Mikoloski puts it:

> *The best thing about working in coffee shops and at home is that you are completely divorced from office politics, and everyone knows they can be brutal.*

He is right: Office politics can be brutal. They are a friction point in many organizations, reducing the effectiveness of teams and increasing project timelines.

Although I might not agree completely with Pavel that the Out of Office worker is "completely" divorced from office politics, I do agree that they benefit from being away from them on a daily basis. Without the need to focus on them as much, the Out of Office worker is allowed to be more productive and more focused on the job at hand.

Reduced Stress—Improved Health

Although I'd love to paint a picture of a stress-free life working Out of Office, that simply isn't true. However, what is true is that the type of stress and the way it is controlled changes dramatically from the in-office worker to the Out of Office worker.

One of the biggest stressors before the in-office worker even arrives at the office is the commute. Whether via public transport or personal vehicle, dealing with commuting increases most workers stress levels at some point in their working week. Whether it is cancellations or delays in service, traffic congestion, or the weather impacting travel, those who travel on a daily basis over any distance to and from work will feel the stress.

Arriving at the office in a stressed state doesn't bode well for a stress-free day or a particularly productive one.

The Out of Office worker, depending on where they happen to be working, is less likely to feel this pressure. Certainly those who work most of the time (or even some of the time) from home enjoy a commute that is like none other. My personal commute most days is two minutes and constitutes me shuffling down the hallway from the kitchen to my office. The only traffic I encounter is one of my cats coming the other way—hardly gridlock!

Co-worker tension is another source of stress for most people working in a corporate environment. Even the most laid back of people can't get along with absolutely everyone. At some point, we all meet that one person that no matter the situation, rubs us the wrong way. This is also true for the Out of Office worker; however, they have the opportunity to deal with it in a different way. It would be most definitely frowned upon if an in-office worker were to scream and shout at a colleague. But an Out of Office worker can take the time to do just that—after the fact. After all, if they are alone at home, then screaming at a wall or even their computer screen affects no one except them.

Even if the in-office worker has the benefit of a private office, screaming in it still doesn't go over well with co-workers. Sometimes things don't require a scream but rather just a change of scenery. As we've already seen from some of the accounts in this chapter, the ability to walk away, to go to the park or a coffee shop, as the mood takes them, is something that Out of Office workers relish.

Simply walking out of the office without an explanation to take a walk in the park would definitely not be seen as professional in an in-office setting, unless you had the most understanding of co-workers and bosses. Of course, the Out of Office worker doesn't have carte blanche to come and go when they like—there are conference calls, video conferences, and other virtual connections to be maintained. However, they do have the freedom to manage their stress in ways that aren't always available to their in-office colleagues.

When a person reduces stress in their life, they are also likely to see an improvement in their overall health. Combine that with the fact that an Out of Office worker isn't based inside a "sick building," and the impact on health increases even more. Now, of course, those who are working from public spaces are still open to all the same and some very different illnesses as their in-office counterparts, but given their lower stress levels they are also likely to be able to combat them better.

Improving the health of employees has numerous benefits for both the employee and the employer: reduced health insurance costs for both, reduced out-of-pocket expenses for the employee (which also reduces stress), and reduced amount of lost productivity due to illness, which in turn reduces stress on co-workers as they are not required to take up the slack of someone who is out sick.

Community Involvement

 Out of Office workers, especially those who are based at home, are able to become involved in their local communities because they aren't spending as much time traveling to and from work.

Being connected to their community makes people feel more grounded and provides them with a sense of stability—stable employees are less likely to look for alternative employment. A stable workforce is a huge benefit to any organization.

In a previous role, where I worked some of my time from an office and some of my time from home, I was able to be a part of the local volunteer fire department. It gave me the opportunity to join in my community, provide a valuable service, and learn skills that were applicable to my job. Leading a team of volunteers into a burning building definitely teaches you how to get the best out of co-workers under stress!

Of course, community involvement doesn't have to be at that level; it can be anything that makes an employee feel more connected to the place where they live. The point is that in allowing the Out of Office employee the ability to set their own schedule, the employer facilitates the opportunity for their employees to do things that are of interest to them. As I mentioned, those activities may well have benefits beyond simply the feel-good factor for the employee: They may well lead to an increase in their skill set that they bring back to the organization, thus benefitting both the organization and their co-workers.

Saving Money

 Whether one is working for a "just me" organization or a large corporate one, the bottom line is the primary driver for making most business decisions. There are considerable cost benefits to having Out of Office workers as part of the make-up of the team.

The costs of heating, lighting, and furnishing an office are a major capital expense for any business. Having fewer individuals to provide those items for reduces the overall expense of a business. Although some costs will always be retained, such as 401k, medical insurance, recruitment, training, and other human resource expenses, by reducing the space required to operate a business, an organization can offset some of those costs. In effect, the organization asks the employee to cover some of the cost by working from home. The benefit to the employee can also be expressed in financial terms. Because they are no longer commuting to an office, the cost of travel is mitigated. If they were rail travelers, the cost of a season ticket (no small sum) is removed. If they were car commuters, the cost savings can be even higher. First of all, the reduced consumption of gas will be a cost saving. In addition, many insurance companies offer discounts to people who drive less than the average 12,000 miles a year, so a home-based worker would be well advised to ask their insurance company about getting a reduction in their premium. Maintenance costs are lowered as wear and tear on the vehicle is reduced along with the mileage.

Food is another area where the Out of Office worker can find cost savings appearing. When an employee is office based, they are often tempted to eat at the company cafeteria or local eateries. A home-based worker is more likely to eat something from their own pantry or refrigerator, something that they have already purchased. This food is most likely to have cost less than its equivalent purchased from an outside vendor, even a subsidized cafeteria.

Clothing can be another area where the Out of Office worker finds themselves saving money. With no suits or formal wardrobe required to work from a home-based office, the need to replace these items on a regular basis is removed or at least reduced. Sleep pants are considerably cheaper than dress pants!

Another area where some save money is childcare. Not having to pay for playschool, a child sitter, or other form of daily childcare can be a huge savings.

Of course, there are some cost increases involving lighting, heating, and cooling, but these are usually more than offset by the savings that are realized. Also, tax benefits need to be considered. If a person uses a part of their home for work, that square footage can be claimed on their tax return. These benefits are something that any corporate HR department will most likely explain and factor into a package for an Out of Office worker. These should also be investigated thoroughly by small and solo-person businesses to see what cost savings can be made over opening formal offices.

Setting Priorities

The ability to adequately set and maintain priorities within the working environment is paramount for in-office workers. The same is also true of those working Out of Office. The difference that exists between the two is usually that an in-office worker has their priorities set for them, often based on the changing demands of the office environment. The distance between the office and the Out of Office worker provides a buffer, a form of insulation, from these types of changes. Although this means that an Out of Office worker cannot typically be used to work on projects that are in a constant state of flux, it does mean that they are usually granted the freedom to establish their own priorities and to a degree manage them.

This freedom comes with a cost, because they are also required to have the maturity and a degree of organizational understanding to see clearly which activities are priorities and which are not. This is one element for determining who is suitable for this type of work style in an organization and who is not. Not all employees can work efficiently with minimal direction. That is not necessarily a failing but rather a particular work trait. Of equal importance is the ability to see the larger picture within an organization, to understand what is a priority now and what is likely to become a priority. Because of the distance between the Out of Office worker and their in-office colleagues, which is more than simply physical, the Out of Office worker needs an almost prescience in order to ensure that they are as responsive as possible.

This is certainly not a trait found in everyone; for example, a junior team member, fresh from college, is unlikely to have the organizational knowledge and big-picture sense to be able to manage the priorities necessary, and it would be unfair to place that level of expectation on them. An employee who has the experience, organizational knowledge, and maturity is more likely to be able to meet the challenge of being an Out of Office worker. Those who are able to manage and maintain their own priorities and juggle the demands placed upon them with the distractions of an Out of Office work style are invaluable to any organization.

Deciding when and, in the case of the Out of Office worker, where to tackle projects is indeed a luxury. I certainly like to know that I am free to decide when I write a blog post, an article, or a chapter of a book or work on a client project as I feel the pull. Writing in particular is not something that I am necessarily going to do on a schedule. Although I have daily targets I always strive to meet, I don't always write at the same time of the day or in the same location. I find that freedom to be very helpful in the creative process. On the other hand, many writers will tell you that there is no such thing as "writers block" and that writing is like any other job; it requires discipline and focus and a desire to produce the product. The author William Faulkner was a major advocate of this approach:

> *I only write when I am inspired. Fortunately, I am inspired at 9 o'clock every morning.*

Client projects tend to take priority for me, if for no other reason than they are paying me to make them a priority. The same is true for those working for a larger organization; provided the work is done and targets and deadlines are met, it is unlikely that anyone is going to check to see what time of day you wrote a report or created a plan for whatever elements you are working on. This can be a double-edged sword, of course. The temptation to work at any and all times, especially when a deadline is looming, can be considerable. For those with other distractions in the household, the ability and freedom to fit work in around the other demands not only provides great flexibility but, on the flip side, provides the opportunity for unhealthy work practices.

It is not uncommon for people to find themselves working in the early hours of the morning to complete projects that are due, and although most people who have been employed in a deadline-sensitive environment will have done this on occasion, the point at which this becomes a habit can have the reverse effect—instead of increasing flexibility and productivity, it can lead to a decline in productivity.

In a previous role where I was an in-office worker, I once found myself creating online content and uploading it to a client website at 3 a.m. I had to be in a client presentation at 9 a.m. the same day to show the progress of the project, and the content was part of that process. I wasn't part of the delay, but being a team member I was part of the solution. This is an example of when all hands to the pumps and the concept of being part of a team are extremely important to the success of an organization.

It is not unheard of, for example, for even the darlings of the startup/tech world to instigate "lockdowns" and require employees to stay at the office until a project is successfully launched; this sometimes taking up to 72 hours. So the Out of Office employee is far from being alone in finding themselves working irregular hours in the current workplace and economy. Of course, a "lockdown" in your own home or a public place is a little unrealistic, and it would be difficult to imagine an Out of Office worker being able to take part in an all-nighter from the road, unless they are in a hotel. However, the fact that they are used to more flexible working times does mean that they are more likely to be open to working outside of traditional hours to meet project deadlines, and that is definitely an advantage in having Out of Office team members.

Setting Hours

 Another benefit of being an Out of Office worker is that of setting your own working hours. That doesn't necessarily mean exactly what it sounds like, though. Rolling into your office space (wherever that maybe) at 11 a.m. might seem ideal, but unless you work in total isolation, it's unlikely that clients or co-workers will be very impressed if you are only available in the afternoons. However, what it does mean is that if you decide that you want to take two hours off in the middle of the afternoon—maybe to take in a matinee showing of a new movie—provided you are meeting deadlines, there is no reason why not. Visits to the doctor's office, parent/teacher meetings, vet visits, and other important errands are all possible and easier with a flexible working schedule.

I know several Out of Office workers who prefer to start work around 5.30 a.m. and get several hours of work completed before co-workers, clients, and so on, start making their way to the office because they feel they can be more productive. Those same individuals will also feel very comfortable taking the afternoon off, or at least a few hours of it, to run errands, read a book, or catch up on other tasks.

Adam Itkoff outlined the benefits to him of setting his own hours:

> *Telecommuting has provided an amazing improvement in life quality. All of the hours that would be spent schlepping to and from work, now goes directly into projects. This reallocation of energy lets me work more effectively and fluidly. As opposed to chunking out hours, "seven to six" for prep, transportation, and work itself, my work becomes the core of my day, but something done with convenience and vigor. It's not just about working in sweatpants (or robes, as preferred) but more so about synthesizing work life and personal life into something enjoyable and creative.*

This level of flexibility has to be understood by both the individual and the organization for which they work. It is easy for this to be abused on both sides. I know individuals who work for organizations who know that they wouldn't be as productive outside the traditional office environment because they would find errands and projects to complete around their home rather than focus on work. That is definitely a potential hazard, especially for the Out of Office worker based primarily from their home.

For the Out of Office worker who is primarily road based, the flexible work hours can be a definite advantage, allowing them time to experience more of the location they are visiting. They can visit clients on a more flexible schedule and feel more independent than their in-office counterparts.

With flexible hours, clock-watching becomes a thing of the past. Why look at the clock unless you have an appointment approaching (and technology can be used to remind you of that)? Time is irrelevant to the Out of Office worker. Certainly I have days in my home office where I wonder why I am feeling ravenously hunger only to find it is 2:30 in the afternoon and I haven't eaten lunch because I was busy writing or working on a client project.

The rhythm of the office is completely different for the Out of Office worker. In the traditional office setting, the rhythm is set by regular events, co-workers arriving to start the day, coffee breaks, lunch breaks, events triggered by types of work that happen at specific times of the day, such as the end of trading. The rhythm for the Out of Office worker is something that they establish. This rhythm will vary depending on their location. For example, if they are in a hotel, their rhythm will be different than if they are working from home. If they are catching a red-eye flight, it will be different than if they are taking an afternoon flight.

Pam Consear shared how important the control of her own hours is to her and shed a slightly different light on the subject:

> I was a school teacher for nearly 20 years before launching my creative services business in 2008. For the first year or so, my favorite part of being self-employed was just being "out in the world" at 10:00 a.m. or at 1:00 p.m. I felt like I'd been a mole underground all those teaching years, practically chained to my classroom from 8 to 4, and it was exhilarating to see what actually went on in the outside world during school hours.
>
> I still get a little thrill from it—it kind of feels like I'm playing hooky every day, since I've only not been in school as a teacher or a student for 10 of my 47 years.

I love that Pam felt that she not only had control over her hours now but that she also felt she was rediscovering the world outside her previous environment.

This is certainly a benefit to the Out of Office worker, seeing the world at different times and from different perspectives than their office-based colleagues. There is only so much you can see through the windshield of a car in commuter traffic.

This lack of routine can be a cause of stress for some individuals; even those who are well suited to the Out of Office work style can feel the stress of not knowing exactly how their day will progress and having much of their day's progression dependent on others. The Out of Office worker traveling to meet a client in another city for an important meeting who finds their flight cancelled with no alternative flights faces more stress than their in-office counterpart who simply has a meeting shifted by a day or to another meeting room. The type of personality required to cope with this type of fluid schedule is very different from one that relishes in the uniformity of their day. Both are equally valid in terms of being able to contribute to the organization, but neither will probably feel comfortable in the other's shoes.

Those whose job requires some form of creativity are often well suited to the lack of rigor and having the ability to set their own hours that can come with Out of Office working. Having an idea at 2 a.m. and being able to flesh it out from home and then deciding to take a nap to catch up on missed sleep does not tend to go down too well in a traditional office environment (unless, of course, the idea makes the company huge amounts of money). However, for the Out of Office worker, this flexibility can be almost heavenly, freeing them from the strictures of having to be effective between the hours of 9 and 5. As anyone who works with, for, or is a creative type, they will understand that imposing those bounds hardly ever works out well.

I am not, of course, trying to imply that all creative types work better Out of Office—far from it. Having a team around to brainstorm and develop ideas with is a huge bonus for the in-office worker. The difference for the Out of Office worker not being constrained by regular office hours works well for those who feel it to be a constraint; many don't and are more than happy with regular hours. As I mentioned earlier in the chapter, the downside of setting your own hours can be that the line between work and home becomes completely blurred.

Jamie Pritchser emphasizes the freedom of choosing her own hours and how that helps with productivity:

> *Like a lot of creative people, I find it extremely difficult to create and be inspired while sitting at a desk between the hours of 9 and 5. Heck, those aren't even the hours I'm most productive. Over the years, I've worked at home, on planes, in cars, on trains, at airports, on beaches, at friends' houses, at restaurants, at bars, in cafes, at parks, and just about anywhere anyone can think of. A change in scenery inspires me both in the moment and then again later, when I can recall what all five of my senses were experiencing at that festival, in that museum, or along that river walk.*

Without a formal office to go to, the Out of Office worker can be tempted to continue working past normal hours, or start earlier, work at weekends, and so on. This can have a detrimental effect on both them and their families or partners.

When is work time and when is home time? How is balance or integration achieved? We are going to look in more detail at work/life integration in Chapter 9, "Time to Go Back to the Office." However, suffice it to say, I do not believe in a work/life balance. In fact, I think striving to achieve this, especially for the Out of Office worker, is far too stressful. Instead, I believe in work/life integration.

Childcare and Bonding

One of the recurring themes when I was researching this book was the ability for Out of Office workers to spend more time with their offspring.

Whether they worked from home, traveled for work, or did both, Out of Office workers with children all agreed that one of the biggest benefits was being able to spend an increased amount of time with their children over the amount they would have had if they were working in a more traditional in-office setting.

Interestingly enough, this theme was raised by both men and women, both feeling that the Out of Office work style gave them increased opportunities for bonding with their children. Whether it was taking the children to school, picking them up from school, or in fact integrating homeschooling into their work life, the opportunities for bonding seemed to be a point of consensus. Although many large organizations offer on-site daycare for their office-based employees, this is not something that smaller businesses can usually afford to offer as an employee benefit. Therefore, the attraction of actually being able to provide your own daycare, which in turn reduces financial outgoings for the Out of Office worker, is a definite benefit, both emotionally and financially.

As Kirsten Westberg pointed out when she shared her experience:

> When I unexpectedly found out I was pregnant with baby number three, the stress of "How will we pay for daycare for a third child?" did not exist. I just knew that I would adjust my working hours around the schedule of a newborn, and we would not have the burden of extra childcare expenses, and I was free to enjoy the surprise instead of feel the weight of what could be seen as a burden to a family on an already tight budget.

It's not just the ability to spend more time with children, but also the quality of that time. The connection becomes more than just childcare. Involving children in what it is you do for a living and making them a part of it is a great way to achieve a bond that those who work solely from an office would find hard to replicate, mostly because when they get home from a day at the office they simply want to put that work behind them and focus their time and attention on family matters.

Of course, having children at home during the work day can be a distraction, but the majority agreed that the benefit far outweighed the cost of having to reorganize their time around the needs of their children. A great example of integrating work with childcare came from Steph Calvert:

The biggest benefit to working at home for me is being here 24-7 for my son, Phil. He doesn't have to go to daycare. He stays in the office with me and gets to see what I do for work first hand! While I'm working on graphic design projects on the computer, I set him up with crayons and paper on the light table so he can "help" me with what I'm doing. Sometimes when I'm inking a t-shirt illustration, he'll ask me to Xerox a copy of the line work for him so he can color it in, coloring book style.

Brigham Young University conducted a study among IBM employees in 2010 and found that one of the benefits for Out of Office workers was what has been dubbed the Mac-and-Cheese effect. Quite simply the opportunity to sit down to a family dinner with the children recharged the adults and benefitted them as much as it did the children. That hour or so not spent commuting but instead spent eating dinner as a family unit allowed the Out of Office worker to relax and separate home from work, even if they went back to their home office after the meal.

Managing the Process

Being Out of Office but remaining part of the flow of information and product is a great challenge; however, it is also part of the benefits. The advances in technology mean that remote working is no longer the challenge it once was. Take, for example, the process of version control for documents. In the past this was dependent on emailing documents between team members, hoping that each person who edited the document annotated what they had changed, and then forwarding the correct version to the next person. Anyone who has ever experienced this nightmare knows how frustrating it is to find that you have spent hours working on the wrong version of a document and having to start again from scratch.

Of course, tools such as Microsoft Word have assisted in this area with features such as "Track Changes," but that is still reliant on the right document being sent.

Tools such as Google Docs and others allow multiple users to work on the same document at the same time and view changes in real time. This makes the process of managing changes much simpler and increases the ability for the Out of Office worker to be a part of and even manage the process, thus leveling the field.

The advent of the "cloud" environments (offsite storage as a service) provided by companies such as Dropbox are also changing the way organizations, even traditional ones, are working. Instead of important documents being stored on individual employees' computers or even shared servers, documents are stored in the cloud, accessible by all those who need them, including those who are working Out of Office. This is incredibly important for those working as part of a team. The ability to collaborate, update, and improve upon documents, plans, and designs is essential. The organization also benefits because of the centralization of work. Rather than pieces of a project being distributed among the teams various devices, the project is centralized. If a device fails or goes missing, the project is still safe and those working on it can continue without interruption.

Those who work for themselves are more usually familiar with managing processes often because they are the only person involved in the process. Even when this is not the case and others are involved, managing a process from home or another remote location is often something Out of Office workers are adept at doing simply because of the nature of their work style. They are flexible, constantly faced with challenges that their in-office co-workers don't face with the same regularity, and they are problem solvers. Those who don't possess these attributes don't usually make for good Out of Office workers and usually find themselves returning to the more traditional office setting.

I am, of course, painting broad strokes in describing the Out of Office worker, and just as each in-office worker possesses strengths and weaknesses, so does the Out of Office counterpart. However, certain traits are common to the successful Out of Office worker that transcend industry and job type and make this type of worker stronger in some areas than their in-office colleagues. Although in-office workers should know how to manage time, work well with others, and oversee processes and workflows, the Out of Office worker *must* master these.

Being managed and managing others remotely can also bring benefits, to both the Out of Office worker and their colleagues in the traditional office. Wes Rogers makes a very good point about those "overheard" moments in the traditional office:

> *I don't overhear managers freaking out like I do when I'm in my cube in the office. This is usually a good thing and helps me be one of the most stable members of my team. In fact, I've even managed small teams remotely. And they didn't have to hear me freaking out.*

The amount of separation between managers and teams offered by Out of Office working can provide a buffer that allows both to benefit by giving time for situations to cool off before being presented. Even when managers have the benefit of being able to close a door to their office and discuss things with an employee, the very fact that the door is closed sends a message to the rest of the office that something is wrong. The fact that a manager can't call an Out of Office employee into their office immediately puts a pause into the process that can often lend time to gaining perspective or allow additional information into the situation that would have otherwise not been included in the thinking.

The same is true when it is the manager who is the Out of Office worker. I have managed remote teams from my home office, and having to take the extra time to aggregate all the information before making a conference call has helped me make better decisions on more than one occasion. This benefit, of having a buffer before reacting, is something that is often overlooked when considering incorporating Out of Office work styles into a corporate environment.

We all like to think of ourselves as being good managers, or at least competent ones, and believe that we would always take the time to consider all angles before reacting, but often, under the pressures exerted by the corporate environment, we are prone to knee-jerk reactions. I am not saying that working Out of Office means that this doesn't happen, but the ability to react immediately is reduced and therefore, as Wes has pointed out, it is more likely that the Out of Office worker or manager is going to be viewed by co-workers as more stable.

Organizational continuity is also more achievable with a distributed workforce.

In 2012, the East Coast of America was blasted by Superstorm Sandy. Lower Manhattan was flooded, and many areas of the Northeast coast were without power. The human cost was considerable; the cost to businesses was huge, with many unable to continue operations for a few days at least.

With a workforce distributed across geographical locations, the risk of this type of disruption is amortized. This is of benefit not just to the employees and the organization but also their customers. Although it sounds heartless, the truth is that if you can't meet your client's deadlines, even with a viable reason like a hurricane, you can and will lose business.

Having a workforce where at least some of the team is not impacted by the event allows for the company to at least limp along until normal operations are restored. That can often be the difference between retaining and losing a client, especially for a small business.

This type of risk reduction can be a compelling argument for employees looking to get employers onboard with the idea of having a telecommuting workforce. It can also be used by organizations as part of their differentiator when pitching for business to clients, especially if the organization concerned is a provider of time-critical services.

Recruitment and Retention

Organizations that offer Out of Office work styles have found that they are more likely to retain those workers than those organizations that don't. The reasons for this are quite simple. If, for example, the spouse or partner of an employee has to relocate for their job, often the other partner will leave their own job as well.

However, if the employer can offer Out of Office working as a solution, they are more likely to retain that person—all other things being equal.

Out of Office work styles also fit with some forms of physical disability better than in-office working. This allows employers to broaden their recruitment reach and include talented individuals in their workforce that they might have previously overlooked because of the logistics involved in modifying existing facilities.

Even offering a blend of Out of Office and in-office working can be a competitive edge when looking at recruiting or retaining talent. Allowing employees the flexibility to work some of the time from home and some of the time from the office, usually on a schedule, allows both parties to benefit from the arrangement without straining the organization if they are not familiar with this type of working arrangement.

It can often be the stepping stone to allowing some employees to be full-time Out of Office team members.

This type of flexibility, especially when viewed through the eyes of employee retention, has additional benefits. As much as corporate organizations have attempted to reduce "tribal knowledge" and introduce knowledge management systems, it remains true that a considerable amount of both strategic and tactical information remains with individual employees.

Retaining these people at points where they might otherwise have moved onto other organizations is obviously a huge benefit to any company. With the right technology, organizational will, and the right people, most organizations can make at least some of their roles location agnostic.

Feels Less Like Work

Let's face it: The opportunity to work from the pool, patio, beach, coffee shop, or any of the other great locations that the Out of Office worker gets to call their "office" is definitely not going to feel as much like work as navigating traffic and working in a cube.

 If it doesn't feel like work, then it is likely to be more enjoyable, and happy people are more productive. The truth is that waking up each day and knowing that your commute is two minutes or less down the hallway, or across the street to a coffee shop, is a lot less daunting than facing a mile-long tailback on the freeway.

The ability to choose to work from your couch, desk, patio chair, or anywhere else feels a lot less constraining than being faced with the grayness of a cubicle wall—even if you have managed to personalize it to a certain degree.

Organizations have to meet legal standards in the workplace, especially when it comes to health and safety. OSHA regulations, for example, stipulate what types of equipment can be used and where they can be used. So that toaster oven in an employee's cube is very likely going to be removed because it doesn't meet with the building code. However, for the Out of Office worker, having a toaster oven in the workplace is perfectly acceptable. Heck, they don't even have to have it in their office; they can leave it in the kitchen.

The DVR is the friend of the in-office worker: Those favorite shows that are on when they are commuting to or from work, the late-night ones that they can't watch because they need sleep, those fill up the DVR. The problem is, when does the viewer get to watch them? The Out of Office worker can enjoy a casual lunch catching up with shows in their DVR queue without concern—as long as they meet their deadlines, who cares if they watch a show during lunch?

How many in-office workers get a text message from their partner every day asking them to stop off on the way home to pick up something from the store? I'm sure tens of thousands of texts like that are sent every day. The Out of Office worker has the luxury of going to the store at times when it is less busy; they are not fighting with all the others who are dropping in on their way home. No, for them the grocery store is a peaceful, uncrowded place to select produce.

All of these benefits contribute to the sensation for the Out of Office worker that what they do feels a lot less like work and a lot more enjoyable than the work style their in-office colleagues endure.

©CasaWeenie.com 2013

3

The Challenges

In Chapter 1, "Why You Shouldn't Try an Out of Office Experience," I outlined some of the reasons why Out of Office working might not be the right work style for you or your organization. I am assuming that if you have made it this far into the book, you have at least decided that there is some fit for you and/or your organization.

In this chapter, I want to consider the various challenges that exist for the Out of Office worker and how they can be overcome. As I've already mentioned, I believe that this style of working requires a particular mindset and that it doesn't work for everyone who tries it. The challenges are myriad and unique to this type of work style; however, the solutions to them are just as unique and, in some cases, creative.

What all the solutions have in common is that they are created by the need to be as productive, if not more so, than office based co-workers, as well as to allow the Out of Office worker the freedom that this work style is meant to enable.

All of us, whether in office or Out of Office, face challenges daily in our work lives; for example, our productivity can be stalled by a co-worker not completing their portion of a project, or a chatty co-worker might drop by our cube and consume an hour with tales of their weekend.

Although the Out of Office worker can relate to these challenges, and has probably experienced them during their working life, if their in-office co-workers have not worked Out of Office, it will be difficult for them to relate to the challenges faced by their Out of Office partners.

To start with, let's examine some of the challenges faced by the Out of Office worker based at home.

Partners, Pets, Children, and Other Demons

 I am extremely fortunate to have a partner who supports what I do for a living and understands the needs of an Out of Office worker for a designated space to call one's own, even if it is shared with guests on occasion.

However, even an understanding partner will, at times, make demands of the Out of Office worker that eat into their work time.

The Out of Office worker, especially one who is home based for the majority of their time, can be seen as neither fish nor fowl; they are neither home full time nor away full time. So what is the harm in asking them to help out around the house while they are there all day?

Denise Snow explains how partners, children, and even neighbors can be dismissive of your job:

> *The biggest challenge I find is that others do not take your work seriously when you work from home. Because you work from home, why can't you do domestic chores, watch their kids and pets, and run errands when you please? Why can't you just pick up your computer and work from just anywhere? This seems to be pretty common perception of my family, friends, and neighbors. Neighbors that ring your door bell and think you have all day to chat, or how about going out to have some fun during the work day? Family that says, "what are you doing tomorrow?" My answer: The same thing everyone else is doing—working!*

It's not just domestic chores that are added to the list; there is always that leaky faucet that needs to be fixed or a set of shelves to be put up. There is a strong likelihood that an Out of Office worker will be involved in the information industry, so the Internet is an integral part of their work. Partners can also see this as a great opportunity to have their own "researcher" at home during the day. "Can you get a quote for car insurance?" or any number of other Internet-based tasks will be offloaded to the Out of Office worker.

Even the most supportive of partners can forget that just because their partner works from home in sweatpants, they aren't necessarily under any less pressure to deliver on deadlines, produce quality work, or deal with all the demands of an in-office-based role.

The illusion of work as leisure given by the fact that showers may be something that are taken in the afternoons, that sweatpants are worn all day, and that some of the office time might actually happen in a coffee shop, doesn't help that blurring of the lines.

It is important for the Out of Office worker to be able to illustrate to their domestic partners that they are, in fact, working each day. If the partner goes out to work each day, they are likely to return home with tales of the work place. For the Out of Office worker, especially the home-based one, they are unlikely to have the same types of stories to tell. However, I believe it is important that they share stories of their work day as well as listen to their partner's stories. These stories provide a point of reference, a context in which the non-home-based worker can place their partner and their day.

I have known home-based workers who were primarily involved in some form of information or creative-based business whose partners had little or no understanding of what it was they did for a living. Images of time spent cruising the Internet, watching daytime television, playing video games, or simply going for coffee were common among their partners.

The fault lies not with the partner, but with the Out of Office worker for not dispelling these myths (okay, so some of us might indulge in these activities from time to time, but not all the time). Communication, as in any other aspect of a relationship, is paramount.

Explaining what the day, week, or month's activities are going to look like to a partner is definitely a way to aid their understanding of what the Out of Office worker does all day at home.

When the Out of Office worker is part of a larger team, this can be a lot easier than for someone engaged in a solo enterprise. I have often answered the question "What did you do today?" with the simple answer "I wrote." It sums up what I did, but it doesn't really help my partner understand what I did.

Even if I were to quantify the writing—"I wrote ten pages of my new book today," which is, of course, more detailed—it doesn't really explain what I did. Is ten pages a lot or a little? Did I do research, or did I just write it all off the top of my head?

Of course, sometimes those details aren't as important as quantifying the tasks accomplished in terms of time. "I spent six hours writing ten pages today" is actually more useful as a response. It provides context. Of course the next question is, "What did you do with the other four hours I was at the office?" Just as if you were an in-office worker being quizzed by your boss, how would you describe what it was you did for those seemingly nonproductive hours?

The home-based Out of Office worker has no commute time to eat up part of their working day. Perhaps a few phone calls or video conferences, but really where did that time go?

I honestly couldn't quantify where that time goes for my own day. Of course, there are the usual Internet distractions, although I try to minimize those. Sometimes it is just a matter of spending time thinking—which is very hard to put into words.

Partners also form an essential part of the support network and are not the only challenge faced by the Out of Office worker. In fact, some share the experience with their partner when they both work from home.

Wes Rogers offered his experience of sharing an office and home life with his wife:

> *Recently we had our first child, and it couldn't be easier. We are both basically right back at work full time, just sharing the duties at home. The change hasn't been that dire—of course, I can't do much feeding as my wife is breast feeding, but, it's nice to know we're there to help each other out.*

With both partners working from home—and in Wes's situation for the same company—they understand the challenges and can provide assistance to each other, relying on each other's strengths.

Other parts of the Out of Office worker's day might be spent dealing with the other distractions that we share our living space with—pets.

We have three cats living with us, and they are a source of amusement, affection, and, of course, distraction. Each one of them has its own personality and its own needs. Any home-based Out of Office worker sharing their space with a pet will understand the distractions that pets provide.

Dogs require walking, or at the very least being let out into the yard; cats will demand attention at the most inappropriate times. It can be hard to concentrate on a conference call while also listening to a cat cough up a fur ball and wondering which room now has an unpleasant mess in it to be cleaned up!

As I mentioned previously, one of our cats enjoys being in on video conferences, if I forget to shut the door to my office. Fortunately, so far, he hasn't interrupted an important client call or a video interview, but it definitely keeps me on my toes knowing that he might put in an appearance at any time.

I have heard tales of home-based Out of Office workers finding their dogs gnawing on cables and disconnecting them from the Internet, cats that sleep on keyboards and change documents while no one is looking, and one case of a collapsing fish tank that destroyed a computer and took with it critical documents!

There is no doubt that sharing your workspace with pets brings a unique set of challenges that few in-office workers ever face (with the odd exception of offices that allow people to bring their dogs to work).

Explaining that the "dog ate my work" to your boss is not quite the same as it was when you were in grade school. These challenges have to be worked around. Securing devices, utilizing cloud backup services, and generally making continuity plans around the possible mishaps that pets can create is essential for Out of Office workers.

Of course, at the same time, for the home-based Out of Office worker, pets can provide a measure of company. Certainly having the cats around me while I am working provides a comforting feeling of not being completely alone all day. The opportunity to take a dog for a walk around the block can help refresh and recharge an individual. Moments like those are one of the big attractions to being an Out of Office worker.

When you're planning an Out of Office work style, pets (either existing ones or potential additions) have to be incorporated into the plan. For instance, a new puppy might be a wonderful addition to the household, but with an Out of Office worker at home all day, guess who will be looking after it while the rest of the family is out at work or school?

The other family members who will have a huge impact on an Out of Office work style is, of course, children. No decisions of the scale involving the setting up of a home office environment can be made without incorporating the needs of children in the home.

From the space that an office takes up, to the daily schedule needs of children, to the length of school vacations—all these things will impact the Out of Office worker based at home to varying degrees.

As we have already seen in Chapter 2, "The Benefits," working from a home office with children in the house can also present opportunities for bonding that would otherwise be missed. However, for every opportunity there are also examples of where work has to be rescheduled to allow for the needs of a child.

I recently saw a post from a friend on Facebook that said the following:

Home Office + Sick Kiddo = No Work Getting Done Today

What happens in a situation like this? What about those deadlines? What about the clients or colleagues who are expecting your input? Of course, this is a challenge that in-office workers face as well. If both parents are present, one of them probably chooses to stay home with the sick child while the other goes to work.

However, when one of the parents already works from home, then the natural assumption is that they will take care of the child. What if the parent is a lone parent? If they don't have access to additional childcare help, then when does that work get done?

For some it simply means having to reschedule work, move deadlines, or otherwise make compromises. For yet others it means burning the midnight oil after a day of nursing their child and playing catch-up through the night. Not an easy task, but one that most parents would do willingly in exchange for being there for their sick child.

Sickness is, of course, not the only time children require a parent's full attention. The parent working from home will also have their available time reduced by the school vacation schedule. The long days of summer can see hours of entertaining children replacing work time. Of course, there are solutions such as summer camps, day camps, and childcare facilities. But let's not forget that part of the appeal of the Out of Office work style is the ability to be flexible. The opportunity to actually spend those lazy summer days exploring a beach with a child or a taking a family trip to the zoo or some other attraction is part of the appeal.

Edward Carroll shared his challenge of trying to operate as the daycare provider and continue to be a productive employee:

> The challenge I found before me was how do I generate leads and engage customers by phone while providing daddy daycare? She would insist on sitting on my lap while I worked. That was difficult because she wanted to talk and pull on my headset while I was on calls. I tried walking around the house while on my calls with using my mobile phone; however, she would follow close behind crying and screaming for me to pick her up. I would usually end up outside on my deck looking back at her through the closed glass door. She would scream because she wanted me to hold her. I felt horrible and frustrated, but I needed to make my calls to generate and close business.

This is a tough situation for any parent to find themselves in. The whole point of working from home for Edward was to spend time with his daughter and yet in doing so he was putting his job at risk. Happily, he and his wife figured out a schedule adjustment that meant everyone, including his daughter, got what they needed, but as they found out, it takes a different kind of thinking to overcome the challenges presented by being an Out of Office worker.

If the Out of Office parent is part of a larger organization, both the worker and the organization need to think through carefully the strategy for coping with these different situations. Although sickness is hopefully short term, school vacations are usually longer and require more of the parent's attention to be devoted to their child or children. Work still has to be completed and deadlines met. Sometimes the only recourse is to simply inform co-workers and bosses that the Out of Office parent will be unavailable while they deal with a sick child. The school vacations will involve other strategies, the most common of which will see the Out of Office parent working at different times than during school days.

I know many Out of Office parents who get up several hours earlier than normal, put in a few hours of work before their school-age children rise, and then spend the day with them. Then, once dinner is completed, they return to their home-based office to put in more hours to ensure that work stays on track.

Shelley Hunter Kukuk explains that structuring her day around the needs of her children has been the biggest challenge to working from home:

> For me, the biggest challenge is having a lack of structure to my day. Because I chose to work at home as a way to be an at-home mom and still help support the family, my primary job is being a mom, which means I am the caregiver, addressing all the needs of the children throughout the day, while also working.
>
> This was significantly more challenging when the kids were all little. Now that they are all in school, I have more time to get things done and can structure my day, but they invariably have needs that I must tend to.

Whether Out of Office workers are working for themselves or working as part of a larger organization, operating on a flexible schedule but still meeting the needs of both the family and their job is a common challenge for all.

Far from being all about luxuriating in the sun by the pool, many Out of Office workers, especially those who are parents, will often find themselves at the very least working irregular hours and in some cases working much longer hours than their average in-office counterparts. Of course, the opportunity to be a part of their child's life during school vacations means that the extended hours are often a cost worth paying.

Interruptions

What about the other demons of the domestic environment? Every Monday at my apartment complex, the maintenance crew washes down the courtyard that our balcony overlooks. It's great that they keep the place so pristine; it's unfortunate that they do it with a power washer. The small engine that powers it echoes from the walls of the buildings surrounding the courtyard; even with the balcony doors shut, it only reduces the sound to an annoying din, certainly too loud to talk on the phone, even in my office.

Leaf blowers and other power tools being used by neighbors or maintenance services have the uncanny knack of being fired up at the most inappropriate times. Of course, the Out of Office worker becomes adept at pressing the mute button repeatedly during calls for just these reasons. Still the unexpected will always happen.

I have been in the middle of a video call and had to halt it to answer the door for an urgent package delivery. Although hardly embarrassing or particularly inconvenient, the unscheduled nature of these types of interruptions can be a nuisance and break the flow of a conversation. As private and secluded sounding an office at home sounds, it is never quite the cone of silence that in-office colleagues think it is.

Mail centers and other facilities can be utilized to minimize even these types of interruptions, and we will look at things that you can (and quite probably) should outsource to make you more efficient later in this chapter.

Of course, in-office colleagues have their share of unexpected interruptions: How many of them have found themselves evacuating a building for a fire alarm, or even a fire drill? Nothing like half an hour spent outside during the winter in a parking lot to wreck the creative flow!

For some reason those interruptions aren't placed on the same level as interruptions experienced by those working Out of Office. Somehow the Out of Office worker, by virtue of the fact that they work in their own home, is supposed to be able to exert more control over their environment than their in-office colleagues. As I discussed in Chapter 2, in some situations that is certainly true, but there are situations over which they have no more control than anyone else.

Again, the best strategy is to plan for these eventualities. I lost power for a few days while living in an apartment a couple of years ago. A construction team had managed to sever a power line or disrupt the power in some manner. My fallback plan was to work from a local coffee shop for most of the day, and use a bookable "reading room" at the local library to conduct video meetings. It wasn't sustainable for a prolonged period of time, but it kept me up and running for the few days that I was without power—and kept me in business.

Having contingency plans in place before the interruption occurs is the only way to achieve something close to the seamless continuity that co-workers or clients will require. It also demonstrates a level of professionalism that those constituents will expect.

Domestic Chores

The temptation for the partner of a home-based Out of Office worker to utilize them to deal with some of the demands of running a home is great indeed. For the Out of Office worker who lives alone, domestic chores can become an escape or even an avoidance tactic from performing work that needs to be done. At a conference I recently attended, one of the speakers stated to the audience that one of the best ways to ensure you have a really clean house was to decide to write a book!

Of course, in any partnership there must be compromise for it to be successful. Does it really impact the work day if a home-based Out of Office worker takes 15 minutes to load the washing machine in the middle of the day, or an hour to run to the grocery store? No, probably not. The only problem is when these tasks become a barrier to productivity. Scheduling time to do them can be a big help. For example, knowing that their work day will have a break around 3 p.m. to do the school run allows for both partners to be certain of who is picking up the children and allows for the Out of Office worker to plan their day accordingly.

When both partners are extremely busy, it can be beneficial to bring in outside help. My partner and I have done this when she has been traveling a lot for business and I have been both traveling and writing with tight deadlines. During these times, we have utilized the services of a cleaner to keep our apartment in good shape—no one likes to live or work in a mess.

It was an additional expense but, after doing the math, we reasoned that it was very worthwhile to allow us both the ability to complete our work and still enjoy some time together and not be spending our time cleaning.

Utilizing additional services to help achieve either domestic or personal goals, thus freeing up time for the Out of Office worker and their partner, where appropriate, can be extremely beneficial.

Services such as TaskRabbit, which is not available in all areas yet, but is spreading rapidly, are allowing people to get more done within the same time frame. TaskRabbit is basically an outsourcing service for any number of jobs, from doing Internet research to picking up dry cleaning or groceries. Jobs are posted by users who need a task completed; they are bid on by "Rabbits," and when the bid is accepted and the task complete, they are paid. Currently only available in Los Angeles, San Francisco, Seattle, Portland, San Antonio, Austin, Chicago, New York, and Boston, TaskRabbit makes getting help a lot easier.

How much a task costs will depend on location and, of course, how much value the buyer ascribes to their time. Picking up dry cleaning in San Francisco, for example, costs about $14. Is that worth it? How much does an Out of Office worker make in an hour and how long would it take them to perform the task themselves? It is important to remember to factor in the cost of actually being away from the desk and focusing on other things; it isn't just the cost of not working but the cost of not thinking about work.

Craigslist and other sites can also be utilized in this way to find additional, non-continuous assistance for various domestic and other tasks that take the focus away from work. This type of "buying time" is part of the Out of Office work style that improves productivity and the quality of the life of the Out of Office worker.

Rather than trying to do everything, the savvy worker is now identifying which areas of their lives they are willing to trade money or time for and implementing a work style that fits their lifestyle better rather than the other way around.

Interruptions range from the slightly inconvenient to the almost catastrophic. I am sure that anyone working Out of Office based from home will have experienced them on all parts of the scale. As I have mentioned previously, the primary focus of this book is information/knowledge workers. For these individuals, work flow is an intrinsic part of what they do. Problem solving, creative thinking, and other knowledge-based tasks are dependent on the ability to start and finish a set of thoughts in one session. Having that flow of creativity interrupted can not only be inconvenient but actually cause the individual to have to reset their thinking and start from square one. Certainly, when I am mid-flow writing, my partner trying to engage me in conversation can be not only an interruption but actually annoying. Depending on how it is handled, it can actually lead to some tense moments, which is the last thing you actually want.

What about the Out of Office worker not based at home?

Broader Challenges

The list of potential interruptions and hazards—delayed or cancelled flights, over-booked hotels, traffic congestion, equipment failure, phone calls, urgent emails that turn out to be not so urgent or important—may seem almost endless. Sometimes there is no alternative but to reschedule meetings or hope that colleagues can provide cover for work that is due.

 Although not ideal, this is where relationship building is such a critical element of the Out of Office workers skill set. They must develop the type of relationships with team members so that these in-office colleagues are willing to provide assistance and not simply let the Out of Office worker flounder and deal with the challenge on their own.

Similarly, building relationships with clients to a degree that enables the unexpected to be coped with in a way that reduces its impact is essential. Although most business professionals will understand if a project or other deliverable is delayed for reasons outside of anyone's control, they are less likely to be that understanding if simple contingencies could have avoided or fixed the problem.

When I travel to events at which I am speaking, I always have three copies of my presentation. One on my laptop, one on a flash drive, and one saved to the cloud. The flash drive and my laptop are never in the same bag. Having seen other presenters find that a file is corrupted or that they have lost the file, I am somewhat paranoid about not having my content with me when I get to the event. Three copies might seem like overkill, but it has saved me on more than one occasion. When, for example, my laptop would not be recognized by a projector and my flash drive would not be recognized by the replacement laptop supplied by the venue, having the files available for download in the cloud saved the day.

It is this type of additional planning that helps the Out of Office worker overcome the different challenges they face because of the nature of their work style.

As discussed in Chapter 2, those who travel regularly as part of their Out of Office role will acquire a wealth of knowledge about the best locations, but even for the seasoned traveler there are new experiences and challenges to be overcome.

Finding Internet connectivity, especially when traveling overseas, is always a challenge. I recently traveled to Hong Kong for a speaking event and, of course, didn't want to incur extremely high data charges by using my phone, but I also wanted to stay in touch, not only with my partner and clients but also with my wider social network.

I discovered, quite by accident, that many cafes, bars, and other public places had unsecured Wi-Fi connections. So by simply sitting in one of these places and having a meal or a drink, I could connect my phone to a Wi-Fi source. These weren't always the most reliable or the fastest of connections, but they were free, which met the requirement I had at the time. Of course, I had a much better, faster, and more reliable connection at my hotel, but I didn't want to spend my entire trip in my hotel room.

Internet connectivity is now one of the most important needs of the business traveler (it is also gaining in importance for leisure travelers as well). A report by the Global Business Travel Association (GBTA) and the online travel and expense management company Concur on business traveler needs conducted in 2011 showed that 79 percent of business travelers carry at least one device to remain connected with their home and family.

Another consideration for business travelers is the unsecure nature of most public Wi-Fi connections. Although they are convenient, and in some cases free, they are potential hazards, including being gateways for hackers. The Out of Office business traveler who is using a company device containing sensitive information is better off using a secure device to connect to the Internet. These devices, such as Mi-Fi devices available from most cellular carriers in the U.S., provide 3G/4G wireless connectivity, similar in nature to that of smartphones. Although not always as fast

as a Wi-Fi connection, they do provide the reassurance of being less vulnerable to
security issues than pubic Wi-Fi access points.

Isolation

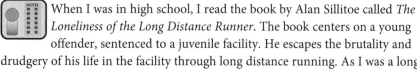 When I was in high school, I read the book by Alan Sillitoe called *The
Loneliness of the Long Distance Runner*. The book centers on a young
offender, sentenced to a juvenile facility. He escapes the brutality and
drudgery of his life in the facility through long distance running. As I was a long
distance runner, the concept appealed to me. I was also an only child, so being in
my own company for extended periods was very natural to me.

Now working from home, I spend most of my days alone. Isolation can be both
a rewarding and a daunting experience for the Out of Office worker. For some,
myself included, being able to control when they interact with others helps with
productivity; for others, the sense of isolation can be overwhelming and hinder
their productivity.

Here's how Kathryn Vercillo expresses it:

> The single biggest challenge for me has been that there is isolation when
> working alone at home. This is how I work best and tends to be what I
> prefer. However, it gets to a point where you are spending way too much
> time alone and this is not only a negative thing socially but also ends
> up being bad for your work because you just don't get the creativity and
> stimulation that you need to be pushing yourself forward in the job.

A lack of inspiration, stimulation, and creativity is definitely going to hinder any
professional's productivity. There are, of course, many ways to overcome this
particular challenge. Networking groups, for example, provide the opportunity to
meet other professionals, many of whom will also be Out of Office workers and
therefore able to relate to the challenges being faced.

JELLY WORKING

Jelly working is a type of co-working provided at no or low cost that has
become particularly popular with both employees and solo-workers looking
for the opportunity to work and socialize with others who are working in an
Out of Office environment and are lacking human interaction. These events
take place anywhere from someone's home to a coffee shop and are designed
as a flexible working environment.

If the Out of Office worker is a solopreneur, then finding others to collaborate with is not only a good business move but also provides a sense of team and human contact.

Hobbies that take place outside of the home are also another way in which the Out of Office home-based worker can increase their level of interaction with those around them. Working out is also a great way to connect with other individuals, either in a class or just in the gym. The sense of being a part of something bigger is a great motivator for many.

All of these methods not only meet the need for social interaction but can also be great sources of inspiration for the creative who is based from home. Whether the contact is professional or personal, simply getting away from the desk and the home office environment and gaining a fresh perspective on tasks is of great benefit to everyone.

Most Out of Office workers already realize this, but even though they understand the benefits, they don't always take it to heart. It can be all too easy for the home-based Out of Office worker to establish routines that focus on keeping them at home, providing them with "reasons" why they shouldn't leave and socialize.

It is worth both employers and partners taking note of this type of behavior and providing opportunities for the Out of Office employee to get out into the wider world.

Support Tasks

Every business professional has two main elements to their role: the actual task and the tasks that support that task. For example, my main job as a speaker is to ensure that I have up-to-date information that I put into my presentations and to create engaging presentations.

However, along with that comes the ancillary tasks, travel, accommodation, contracts, invoicing, and so no. These tasks can be extremely time consuming and distracting, taking my attention away from the primary task.

One popular solution for busy professionals, both those who work for themselves and those who work for larger organizations, is to employ the services of a virtual assistant (VA). Finding a virtual assistant has become easier with the increasing number of those now performing the role. The hard part is finding the right virtual assistant for your needs.

Typically VAs have a minimum number of hours per week requirement, so before engaging one it is essential to have a clear idea of what it is they are being hired to do. The clearer the requirements, the better the relationship will be and the more satisfied the Out of Office worker will be with the results.

If travel is a large part of the role being performed by the Out of Office worker, having someone else book travel and make all the necessary arrangements can be a great timesaver. If research is a supportive part of the role being performed, then having a VA conduct the research and provide the information can greatly reduce project timelines.

Of course, all this comes with a cost. VAs are not cheap, nor should they be: They are, in their own right, professionals who are running a business, and they should be valued as such.

Again, as with any other form of outsourcing of tasks, it is a question of balancing the opportunity with the cost. Does the use of a VA free up useful time that can be better expended on more productive tasks? Also, who pays? For the solopreneur, that answer is simple: They do. But for the employee of a larger organization that can be a more difficult question.

Hiring an individual to conduct tasks that are not directly related to work, but provide a benefit to the organization such as booking travel (for those who work for organizations too small to have their own travel department) can be negotiated. However, hiring an individual who is conducting research on behalf of an employee, even if the research is generic in nature; for example, finding the contact details of potential prospects can be wrought with hazards. Is the VA performing a work-for-hire role? Are they under any form of confidentiality agreement? What happens to the data after it has been collected?

Before deciding to hire a VA, any employee of an organization would be very well advised to discuss it internally with their employer and discuss the pros and cons of such a hire.

For some, hiring a VA to handle the non-work-related tasks makes perfect sense. For a busy Out of Office employee who needs someone to stay on top of making bill payments, managing personal social media platforms, booking vehicles for services, and so on, all of these tasks can be handled by a competent VA and free up time for more productive tasks.

Technology

The solopreneur has both the advantage and disadvantage of being their own IT department. They get to select and maintain their own IT infrastructure. The upside of this is that they make the decisions about what type of equipment should be used, where files are stored, and what type of security should be used. The downside is that they are responsible for all of this; therefore, if something goes wrong, they have little or no choice but to either fix it themselves or call in a professional, which can be very expensive.

Unless they happen to be running an IT consultancy from their home, most solo-preneurs will have limited knowledge about the best ways to set up their home business IT infrastructure. For many, it is simply a matter of buying what they can afford, and setting it up in the way that the instruction manual showed them. Beyond that, they simply hope that it continues to work in the way that it is supposed to.

The Out of Office worker who is part of a larger organization usually has the benefit of the support of an IT department. They make the choices about the type of equipment, how it should be set up, and how it connects to the organizational network.

 This is also one of the challenges. A large organizational IT department is supporting the majority of employees who are "in office." Those who fall outside of this norm present a unique set of problems and are often deprioritized because of it.

Many organizations only allow access to the company IT infrastructure via a virtual private network (VPN) connection. These are notoriously slow, cumbersome, and unreliable. Even working for small organizations I have had to utilize these connections, and they were always a source of frustration. The Out of Office employees I know who are still forced to use them find them no different.

This can act as a barrier to obtaining information necessary to perform a role, or at least obtaining it in a timely manner. This then becomes a source of frustration for both the Out of Office worker and their colleagues. The in-office co-workers have no problems accessing files; they simply navigate to the appropriate network location and open them.

For the Out of Office worker things are rarely that simple. From complex encryption password generators, to multiple logins, to discovering the fact that a particular network location is not viewable from outside of the network, the challenges can seem endless.

If an IT department is equipped to provide individual support to Out of Office workers, this can certainly alleviate some of these issues—but not all IT departments are.

Many Out of Office workers are stuck on hold with their own IT departments as though they were calling a business help line. This does nothing to break down the barrier between Out of Office and in-office workers. It is an added frustration for the Out of Office worker but an unfortunately necessary one given the nature of most organizational IT infrastructures.

Beyond developing good relationships with the IT department, there is little that can be done to overcome these barriers because protecting the infrastructure is the primary concern of the IT department, not making access easier for Out of Office employees.

Relationship Building

 I've mentioned several times throughout this chapter the importance of relationship building and how I see it as key to solving/overcoming many of the challenges faced by the Out of Office worker. It might come as a surprise then to find that according to the 2012 Virtual Teams Survey Report – Challenges of Working in Virtual Teams, 79 percent of Out of Office workers cite "insufficient time to build relationships" as their number-one challenge with the work style.

That number should be of great concern to any organization considering implementing (or those who have already implemented) Out of Office working. Organizations run on the foundation of internal relationships.

The fact that they are removed from the office means that they lack the informal opportunities to form deeper relationships. No hallway conversations, no shared tables in the cafeteria, no vending machine chats, no shared walks across the parking lot to the car for the evening drive home.

These informal meetings are where many in-office relationships develop and an increased understanding of co-workers is achieved. Regardless of the number of video conferences, instant message chats, and phone calls, the spontaneity of the informal meeting cannot be replicated.

Yet, without these deeper relationships the Out of Office worker is hampered in overcoming their challenges: a Catch-22 situation if ever there was one. Again, part of the solution to this is to ensure that the person taking on an Out of Office role is both well versed with the organization and well established in their role within the organization. Another solution is to phase in the transition from in-office to Out of Office working. Start with one day a week and progress, perhaps over the period of a quarter to five days. This at least gives both the employee and their co-workers time to test the arrangement and develop coping strategies for different situations that arise without a complete disconnect between them.

The same survey mentioned earlier also reported that 71 percent of respondents cited "lack of participation" as a major (number-three) challenge. Combine these two, and you have a recipe for a loss in productivity. Obviously they are connected, but without established relationships and the ongoing investment in them, it would be hard to feel included in the organization rhythm.

A lack of participation leads to feelings of disenfranchisement, and that, in turn, leads to employee turnover. Given the cost of replacing key employees (which, by default, Out of Office workers should be), this can be expensive for an organization in more than just financial terms.

Perhaps the biggest challenge exists in the strategy and planning for organizations implementing Out of Office working. The focus tends toward the technological solutions that will allow the maintenance of connectivity and misses the human element and how that connectivity will be maintained.

Although some of the onus for maintaining the connection rests with the employee, the responsibility of the organization to ensure that there is a continuity of relationships and communication cannot be overstated.

Planning for Out of Office employees to make regular visits to the physical office, and in some instances for a prolonged period, can definitely be of benefit to both sides of the equation. I know some Out of Office workers who work on one coast of the U.S. while their peers work on the other. Obviously this type of distance means that a day visit to the office is not only impracticable but logistically impossible. In one instance, the employee will visit the parent office for a week, sometimes once a month or once every six weeks.

Although this arrangement means upheaval at home for the employee, it does ensure that they stay more connected with their peers and allows them to build, establish, and maintain relationships. This might appear to be defeating the purpose of having Out of Office employees, but in a blended workplace (one consisting of both in-office and Out of Office team members) it actually makes a lot of sense.

Where things can be more difficult and costly is when the entire team is working Out of Office. Geographically dispersed teams are not as logistically challenged as they once were. With the technology now available, video conferencing and other collaboration tools make this type of team structure very workable. However, bringing all the team members together is still the same logistical challenge that it ever was.

Finding a destination that is not overly onerous on any one member of the team, that doesn't break the bank, and provides an environment that allows for a productive time together, is no easy task. The cost of these types of trips have to be factored into the operation costs for the business, and for smaller businesses this can be an overhead that seems very unattractive.

I have seen this type of team meeting work extremely well, though—especially when organized efficiently, and that is ultimately the key. Ensuring that those traveling to the meeting know exactly why they are meeting, what the objectives of the meeting are, and any expected outcomes—which is not really any different from a properly organized in-office meeting. The advantages of the Out of Office team meeting is that the setting doesn't necessarily have to be a formal setting.

I recently saw a friend who operates an agency of Out of Office–based team members hold a company meeting in Mexico. Although I wasn't privy to the meetings, I am sure they were productive, but at the same time it was also an opportunity to bond and establish and strengthen the friendships that brought the team together in the first place.

This isn't something all organizations would be capable of making happen or necessarily want to, but for certain groups of individuals it provides both a work and play environment that builds the overall strength of the team—something the organization and its clients benefit from.

This type of bonding exercise is not uncommon in in-office organizations. From outward bound courses to paintball and other leadership/team-building exercises, organizations of all sizes recognize the need for bonding experiences outside of the workplace.

In one of my previous roles at a company headquartered in India, we held senior management meetings at a yoga retreat in the Indian countryside. It was an opportunity for both offshore (U.S. and European) and onshore (India) employees to spend time together, work on their communication skills, understand culture differences, and work on team building.

These trips were extremely successful and helped the company achieve rapid growth while at the same time keeping everyone connected.

Although this all seems great for larger organizations, what of the solopreneur? Without a team, they obviously don't face the same challenges as their team-based peers; however, taking refresher breaks that help them achieve efficiency improvements, recharge them, and perhaps add additional skills to their portfolio is still an important need.

So where do they go? Are there vacation centers for solopreneurs that cater to those looking for some kind of bonding experience and that will allow for an exchange of thoughts and increased education? Although there might well be this type of vacation available (although I wasn't able to find one during the research for this book—business opportunity someone?), the nearest things I have experienced to this are certain conferences.

A conference doesn't seem like it would be the place to recharge, reinvigorate, and educate, but there are some that are particularly aimed at the solopreneur and recognize the challenges of working Out of Office, particularly for those working from home.

With a little research and outreach, it should be possible for most solopreneurs to find a conference or two that caters to this need and provides opportunities for them to get the type of experience that might have previously been thought of as the realm of the larger organization. The extra effort required of the solopreneur after attending this type of event is exactly the same of their peers who work as part of a larger organization. Having experienced the in-person connection, they must strive to ensure that time and distance do not diminish the connection established and try to ensure that the style of communication they achieved face-to-face is replicated, as far as possible, in the remote communications.

This means taking the time to do things such as reading emails more than once to see through the written word to the sentiment. Some people are better at communicating in writing than others, and emails can be dashed off while the person is concentrating on several other tasks at hand. The recipient of the email doesn't have that context necessarily, and what was intended as just a quick note can be interpreted as being curt or even abrasive.

This takes time, perhaps more time than we are used to taking with email, but those extra few moments can be the difference between strengthening or weakening a relationship. There is, of course, a responsibility on behalf of the sender to try and think before hitting Send about how the recipient might misconstrue the message. That is a skill that all email users should acquire; however, given that business moves at the speed it does, it is unsurprising that many never quite manage this.

I will sometimes use a third, unconnected party to read an email that I am unsure of the content of. If I find it abrasive, is it the sender or is it me? In the past, I would just respond in the way I thought was appropriate. However, to my own cost, have found that time, distance, and even cultural differences have led to misunderstandings. Now I find that sending the odd email to a friend and asking for their interpretation reduces the angst and helps prevent those "shoot from the hip" moments.

As most of us appreciate, good communication is the core to building, establishing, and maintaining personal and professional relationships. Working Out of Office and being away from the daily proximity of co-workers, clients, and so on, can sometimes lead to a reduced effectiveness in this core skill, and that is something that anyone considering (or who has already adopted) this work style must consider and pay attention to.

Accountability

Employees of organizations, large and small, understand the concept of accountability. One of the most common ways that employees are reminded of this organizational responsibility is the annual review. Some organizations do these well; others less so. Whichever way they are conducted, the annual review is the point at which an employee discovers how they are performing to expectations and whether or not they are going to move up, stay put, or move out of an organization.

There is an inherent level of accountability when working as part of an organization. An employee is accountable to managers, co-workers, and others. This accountability acts as a guiderail for employees. From work ethic to personal behavior, accountability is often the invisible boss looking over the shoulder of an organizational employee.

What of the Out of Office worker, especially those who are solopreneurs? Of course, there is a level of accountability imposed by working with clients. Missing deadlines, not delivering on promises, or delivering a low-quality experience is a surefire way to go out of business. But what about goal setting and other aspects of accountability? There is no annual review for the solopreneur, no career path per se that provides an indicator of professional progress. Of course, the bottom line provides some indication of achievement, but that is impacted by many factors, not just the performance of the individual.

One way around this is to find a friend or business partner who will help with accountability. I have encountered some solopreneurs who form accountability groups. They overcome one of the biggest fears of this type of group, that of revealing proprietary information by creating non-disclosure agreements between members of the group to avoid conflict-of-interest situations and thereby creating a "safe space" in which thoughts can be shared.

By setting public goals and having others with whom you share progress can be a helpful way to overcome the sense of a lack of accountability. Solopreneurs in particular relish challenges; after all, if they didn't they wouldn't be working for themselves. Without goal setting and accountability for those goals, it can be easy to miss the opportunity to measure oneself and professional progress.

In an organizational setting, it is fairly common to celebrate achievements, large and small. Recognition from co-workers, bosses, or even clients and customers are cause for celebration. Without co-workers, those moments can be few and far between, and when they do occur they can be hard to celebrate. An accountability partner or group can provide that opportunity.

Even if it is only sharing some good news with an accountability partner over coffee, the sense of sharing a success can be inspiring and a motivator to meet the next set of goals. There is much to be said for the "Atta boy" and its impact on the individual and their performance. The interesting side-effect of this is that it is not only the person sharing the success that feels motivated. The person hearing the news shares in that motivation and can be inspired to increase their own efforts in meeting their next goal.

I know of writers who reward themselves with non-work-related treats for completing chapters or reaching other milestones. Perhaps they get to take in an afternoon movie, or spend time playing a video game. Whatever motivator works for them and allows them to meet those goals is a way of keeping track, being accountable, and making progress.

©CasaWeenie.com 2013

Working from Home

Working from home is the most common location for those following the Out of Office work style. The Bureau of Labor estimated that in 2010, 23 percent of all full-time employees worked from home and 64 percent of all self-employed workers worked from home.

 That is a lot of people who have adopted this lifestyle and who are making space in their homes for business.

Strangely enough, this isn't a new phenomenon; as much as we like to imagine the Internet as having created a new way of doing everything from working to shopping to staying connected with friends and family, much of what we think of as new is in fact ideas recycled from an earlier, simpler time.

Working from home used to be referred to as the "cottage industry." In a time before mass transit and privately owned automobiles, when walking or traveling on horseback were the only modes of transport available, most people worked from or near their homes.

Bakers, tailors, weavers, apothecaries, and the other craftspeople essential to the running of a village or small town lived and worked in the same space. Only the inexorable pull of urban drift changed the mode of living and working in separate spaces. From this was born the commuter lifestyle that so many are now reverting from, choosing instead to combine both work and domestic life in the same space. If anything, the Internet has made the broader world into a large village, and many are finding that the best way to adapt to the Internet age is to think in terms of village/small town life rather than the metropolitan lifestyle that was seen as the future only a few decades ago. The difference is that your neighbors may well be thousands of miles from you, or even in another country, so physical proximity plays much less of a role in defining this new village. Instead, the village is defined by relationship proximity—in other words, how close an individual feels to another individual, through shared experiences, shared world views, and shared goals. This is, of course, where social technology has changed what we perceive as our village. I look in more depth at technology in Chapter 6, "Getting Organized," but in general terms, the Internet and social technologies in particular, such as Facebook, Twitter, LinkedIn, and Instagram, have allowed people to create a village of their own choosing, which in turn has enabled individuals to pursue the Out of Office work style who would have previously been unable to do so for fear of total isolation.

Of course, this is nothing new for occupations outside of the information industry. Many individuals and small groups have worked from their homes for hundreds of years and continue to do so. It is only a new experience for the information worker, a relatively new occupation when measured against the total scale of human industry, that is finding the ability to move home with their work.

The ability to access the Internet is the primary requirement for the majority of information workers. As the telecommunications carriers have spread their high-speed networks across the land, particularly in the U.S., areas that would have previously been out of reach for the information worker are now viable as both home and workspaces.

Although it is true that much of rural America still does not benefit from quality high-speed Internet access, and many are still using "dial-up" connections, these numbers are declining. This inevitable spread of access poses the question of whether we will eventually witness a rural drift—a reversal of the urban drift that led so many to abandon small communities in favor of the big cities. Certainly the barriers to living in those communities are falling, and as some of them see an influx of affluent information workers, their infrastructure has to (and in many cases does) improve to accommodate the demands and expectations of their new residents.

Katie McCaskey, the Urban Escapee, has written about the potential that a rural drift offers. She posits the following in her Micropolitan Manifesto (http://urbanescapee.com/micropolitan-manifesto):

> Micropolitan renewal is our best chance for economic growth and environmental repair. Renewal of our smallest cities guards against suburban sprawl and the continued destruction of farmland, habitat, and open space.

This is just one of the multiple impacts that Out of Office workers, especially those who are home based, are having on the broader world. It is important to realize that this work style is not just about individuals being happier but the economic and other impacts it has on the broader community. It has the potential to change the economic landscape of small cities and other areas that have typically not been able to attract higher wage earners because of commuting distances.

Of course, not all Out of Office workers choose to abandon the city just because they are able to work from their home. Many choose to continue the metropolitan lifestyle and take advantage of being able to access its amenities at times when the other residents of the city are unable to, such as the middle-of-the-afternoon workout at the gym, grocery store shopping in the middle of the morning when the store is empty, and so on.

As we discussed in previous chapters, it is the flexibility of working when you want (within reason) that is one of the most appealing factors in working Out of Office from home.

So if the choice has been made to bring work home from the office on a permanent or semi-permanent basis, where should it reside? How much space is required to effectively operate, and what sacrifices are going to be made to accommodate the business? Of course, much of this depends exactly on the type of work being conducted, the original domestic environment, and the available space therein.

As with the majority of this book, I focus on the information worker whose primary tools are a phone, a computer, and Internet access. For the most part, these workers require a minimal footprint when compared to other Out of Office workers.

Where in the Home?

Obviously the total available square footage is the determining factor for how much space can be cannibalized for a workspace. According to the International Facility Management Association, in 1994 the average office worker had 90 square feet of personal space, but by 2010 that had shrunk to 75 square feet.

By that measure I am absolutely swimming in space: The spare room, which I have co-opted at home for my office, is 120 square feet. That puts me on a par, if not slightly above, the space afforded to senior managers at Fortune 500 companies. Perhaps I have already achieved the "corner office" without knowing it. Of course, the reality is that although this room is my office, it is also the spare room, with a fold-out bed in it, and when we have overnight guests they become the priority for the room and I am evicted. My workspace shrinks from the luxury of 120 square feet to whatever corner of the couch or the dining room table I can commandeer.

This is the reality for a lot of Out of Office workers who are home based. Some, however, do manage to carve out permanent places for their work space.

Mandy Vavrinak, owner of Crossroads Communications, shared how she was fortunate enough to convert a space specifically for her needs:

> Three years ago, we deliberately chose a new home with a great "formal living room" right off the front of the house. I remodeled it exactly the way I wanted it and developed a fabulous office space at home. It's spacious enough for two large desks so my assistant can work from my office, too. It has client meeting space as well, so I can do pretty much anything I need to do from it.

Not everyone who works from home has the luxury of dedicating a room or particular area as an office only. Most Out of Office workers have to compromise and work around the needs of those they share the space with, whether that is roommates or relatives.

Adrienne Asaro of Infinite Impressions explains that her home office isn't at the point where she is completely happy with it yet:

> I love that I have my own room to organize my business better. I manage social media marketing and web development for four businesses and I needed a place where I could keep all their files separate and work on their projects separately. What I hate about it is that the room doesn't have an office feel yet. It still feels like itself home and not quite a professional feeling atmosphere. I can't quite put my finger on it; however, I've hired a business advisor to give me tips on organization and management tips on how to help with these issues.

The lack of an "office" feel is a common thread among Out of Office workers who are home based. It can be hard to restrict oneself to an office when it is next to the kitchen or living room and not want to spill into the residential part of the home.

Where the workspace is placed has some common needs. There is usually a need for some form of privacy—a door that can be closed or at the very least a screen that can be used to segment the workspace from the living space.

Thursday Bram of Hypermodernconsulting.com raises another consideration for selecting the space to be used for a home-based office:

> I also feel that taking a full room is a good idea whenever possible. I'm still negotiating with my family as to how much space I get in our new home, but being able to close off the office is usually a good idea. It also dramatically simplifies taking the home office deduction on my taxes.

Depending on your location, the tax implications of working from home can also have an impact on the decision. Having a door that can be closed and therefore clearly delineate the office space can definitely make calculating the amount of square footage used as a home office for tax purposes a lot easier.

Lighting is very important. My office is an internal room, with no natural light, so it's important for me to have several different lamps in the office so that I can adjust the lighting depending on what I am doing, the time of day, and even my mood.

Natural light is important for a lot of people: Many of the contributors who sent me stories about their own home offices emphasized how important it was to them to have windows that let in light and through which they could feel connected with the world.

Lori McPherson works with a stationery company that specializes in items that feature rescue dogs, called Hooray For The Underdog. For her, the choice of location in the home was clear from the outset:

> We turned our third bedroom into a home office. Before we ever moved in, it was my favorite room in the house. It's the bigger of our two guest bedrooms, so I knew it could hold more furniture. It has a large window and I think it just has a great vibe. I knew I needed a great workspace that felt cozy enough to use as living space on occasion but also felt like a place to get things done! We bought a sleeper sofa so that we could still use it as a "bedroom" but that would also double as a place to sit and take calls!

Briana Miriani, who is a realtor and also runs an online business called The Merci, echoed this sentiment, highlighting the thing she liked most about her home office:

> The thing I like most about it is the view; not spectacular, but it's got a big window with a view out into my backyard with some very nice trees, and it gets really good light. It keeps me from feeling trapped!

That feeling of being trapped at home, having no physical separation between work life and home life, is an important factor to take into consideration when placing the home office. When the office is too convenient, it can be difficult to switch off fully and in effect become a 24/7 worker, which, although it might seem ideal for an organization is usually detrimental to both personal health and performance in the longer term.

Mary Baier, a CPA who works from home, finds that even with a dedicated space, being available 24/7 is almost something that her clients expect because she works from home:

My office is 20-by-20 and is on the side of my home. I chose that so customers wouldn't have to go through my home, and it gives me more privacy. I purchased a desktop PC, desk, copier, several printers, a small table and chairs, filing cabinet. My office has lots of closet space for supplies. I have a large church bench for client seating. I have a separate bathroom for clients and a handicap entrance. The office space is just perfect. I prepare taxes, financial planning, and notary services full time. The only drawback is you are at the mercy of customers 24/7, even though you have a sign "by appointment only."

Graphic designer Faith Amon, whose work-from-home lifestyle was featured on MSNBC, also wants the room with the largest windows to avoid that "trapped" feeling:

I've been in business for several years now and have moved houses several times. Each move I sought out the room with the biggest windows so I wouldn't feel trapped inside all day (even though I am—sigh).

I've configured our desks so that we get to look outside at the plants and the butterflies, and I think it is important to our mental health.

Taking into account personal mental health, which I alluded to in Chapter 1, "Why You Shouldn't Try an Out of Office Experience," is something I believe to be crucial when working Out of Office, especially working from home. Not just from the aspect of whether you are the right personality type for working from home but also whether you can cope with the feeling of being "trapped" at home. After all, for most people their home is a refuge, the place they come back to, the place they escape work.

When work life exists inside the same physical location as domestic life, there has to be ways to clearly delineate between the two, not just for the individual but also for the people who share the space.

Ruksanah Hussein, an independent business communicator and green business founder, works from her living room. I wondered how she managed to delineate between what I imagine is a fairly central area to the family and her work space.

This is how she does it:

My husband works outside the home, and I have no children or other dependents living with me. So I pretty much have my place to myself. I follow a pretty strict work schedule: 9 a.m. to 1 p.m. morning hours, then lunch for an hour, and 2 p.m. to 6 p.m. evening hours. Anything that

constitutes home life happens either before 9 a.m. or after 6 p.m. And I
do not watch television during the day or have neighbors or friends liv-
ing close by that would drop in to say hello.

So even utilizing a space that many might be perceived as being central to family living, it is possible to delineate between a work space and domestic space if you are disciplined enough.

Office Contents

Having found the right space for you in the available space and having gained agreement from those with whom you share the space, what are you going to put in this "office"? Of course, for any information worker, the first answer is going to be a computer.

Although that is an expected answer, there is a lot more that has to go into that office space to support the computer, even though that might be the central tool to the space and to the work conducted in it.

At the very minimum, the office is going to need power, a desk and chair, and some form of lighting. From there, the needs build out quickly: storage, accessories, and other organizational tools. Pretty soon what appeared to be ample space can become crowded with "essentials" and take on the appearance of a storage room for an office supply company rather than a daily use work space for an Out of Office worker.

It is not uncommon for home-based Out of Office workers to start from simple, almost humble beginnings and gradually build out over time. Certainly that is what happened with me. As Jeff Zbar with ChiefHomeOfficer.com shares, that was his experience too:

> *Though I started with a length of kitchen countertop affixed to legs*
> *built of 2-by-12 lumber, today my workspace is a desk custom-built to*
> *accommodate my office and work needs. It has ample, hidden storage in*
> *drawers and cabinets; a wire chase for all the phone, power, and Internet*
> *cords and cables; an under-desk enclosure for the CPU; and is designed*
> *at the right height for ergonomic comfort.*
>
> *Speaking of ergonomics, I may skimp on some things—like used file cabi-*
> *nets and home-build shelves—but I have never skimped on an ergonomic*
> *chair. Positive posture is essential to long hours spent at the desk.*

Jeff makes a good point about identifying what is important to being able to sustain the Out of Office work style over what might seem nice to have.

I'm going to go into more depth about the difference between the two in Chapter 7, "Rule Setting." Let's just say that it can be all too easy to focus on the shiny things and spend money where it is less important.

What any one person may deem as necessary may not be the same as another, although the essentials tend to stay the same for all information workers. As I've already mentioned, a connection to the Internet is usually top of the list, immediately after the computer. Without it, an information worker would find it extremely hard to perform their role from home, or the road for that matter.

I personally still prefer a desktop machine in my office; I also have a physical connection to the Internet connected to it. I have a laptop that I also use primarily when I am on the road; it is connected wirelessly to the network and then to the Internet. I guess I am old school enough to want the larger box as the office machine. I also use two monitors to allow me to split my focus between work and social without confusing the two.

My main monitor is where I put Microsoft Word, email, and certain Internet browser windows. Everything else, everything that can be classified as entertainment, goes on the other monitor. This includes music as well as Internet browser windows with Twitter, Facebook, and so on. Separating the two allows me to know where my focus is, because I physically have to turn my head slightly to use the second monitor. If I find myself becoming too distracted, I can simply turn that monitor off and just focus on the main monitor.

When Haralee Weintraub of Haralee.com chose her home-based office, she made it an exclusive space for her business:

> I chose a back bedroom for my office, 11-by-12 feet. There are two desks, two computers, two desk chairs, two book shelves, one four-drawer file cabinet, one printer/fax, and one landline phone. The entire room, including the closet, is office-related materials. The office is used for business, not for family use.

It is interesting to see that Haralee has been able to clearly delineate her office space and makes it clear that it is not for family use.

When an office space contains so many items that can be utilized by other family members, it can be hard to ensure that line is respected. For example, John Miller of Miller Marketing shared the trials he faces with his wife and children:

One other thing that can be extremely frustrating is the fact that my family thinks my desk is a dumping ground and that my office supplies are there for everyone's taking. I just had a conversation with my family that my office supplies (pencils, pens, stapler) are not for the taking. Trying to start my work day without pens or pencils can be seriously frustrating.

I'm sure many of us have been through that experience while working in a traditional office environment of co-workers "borrowing" items from our desks or cubicles. When I last worked in a traditional office environment, it was not unusual to return to my cubicle from a meeting to find that my chair was missing and that it had been dragged to an adjoining cubicle so that a couple of co-workers could have an impromptu meeting. Although that can be frustrating, having your limited resources in your home office being commandeered by family members is probably even more frustrating.

Once I started working out of our spare room, I found that, for some particular reason, it is the most effectively cooled room in the apartment. Although this has its advantages at the height of the Texas summer, it's less of an advantage in the fall and winter as the temperatures start to drop.

I don't want to heat the whole apartment just to stay warm in my office, so I end up wearing an increasing number of layers to work in the office. Even those who have adapted part of their home as a permanent office find the challenges of something as simple as controlling the temperature a factor to be worked around.

Eric Nagel of Eric Nagel & Associates has a dedicated space in his home. It happens to be a converted attic space, which has brought with it some challenges:

My office is in our walk-in attic, the third floor of our house. It's approximately 200 square feet, and sits in the front dormer, so I have a nice big window overlooking the street. I specifically bought the desks to give me a u-shaped desk, which wraps around the inside of the dormer. I like that the office is on its own floor, which keeps things a bit quieter when my kids are home. However, heat rises, so it can get quite warm in the summer. Also, because it's technically an attic, there's no heat up here, so in the winter I'm typically bundled up, or I open the door and let some heat rise up.

Eric specifically wanted that space for the view and the space it offered. He even bought a desk to fit that space specifically, but even with those advantages he still faces some of the challenges that a converted space poses over a purpose-built space.

One of the other reasons to have a dedicated space for some people is the need to accommodate clients. I have never had to meet with clients in my home office. I prefer to meet at their offices because it tends to increase their comfort level. However, for some this is not a practical solution, and for others still it is just a preference.

Having a client sit on the end of a guest bed while you discuss business might not provide the best of business impression, so for those who meet clients in their home, a dedicated, nonshared space is very important.

Shel Horowitz, green marketing/publishing consultant, copywriter, and author of eight books, provided a description of his workspace, which I have to say sounds Sylvanian in the way he outlines the space and the view he has. Shel emphasizes why he choose the particular room he did with his clients in mind:

> Since we moved to our current home in 1998, I've worked from the former parlor of a 1743 farmhouse on a working farm in the Pioneer Valley of Massachusetts (my neighbors have 400 cows and 50 chickens). I chose this room because not only does it have a magnificent view of the mountain behind our house and some of the farm fields, but it's also directly off the front entrance, and therefore clients don't need to walk through the living areas unless they need the bathroom.

Shel obviously realized that providing easy access to his office, not only for him but for his clients, was going to be a primary factor in the choice of his office space and how he laid it out. He goes on to list the essential items in his office:

> ...an ergonomic (Balans-style) backless typing chair, a multifunction printer/scanner/fax, the latest in a series of Macs dating all the way back to 1984, and a broadband Internet connection.

The ergonomic chair was a common inclusion in the stories people shared with me—from the Aeron chair to many other forms of ergonomic chair, the need for a comfortable place to spend long hours at the desk was a common thread.

Desks, on the other hand, ranged from a piece of kitchen countertop through student-style desks from places such as IKEA to more elaborate purpose-built designer items. Of course, what you are willing to spend on your desk is likely to be a function of your available funds. I picked up my lawyer's desk in a consignment store for a fraction of what a similar piece would have cost new. It is a wonderful piece of solid furniture, one that I think will probably outlast me.

Beyond the practical items in an office, gadgets were the next most included item when people shared with me what they had in their offices. I have to confess to being a geek and loving technology. I try very hard not to buy gadgets for the sake of buying them but rather to ensure that they have a purpose and provide a solution to a business problem. Still, there always seems to be some things that just seems to accumulate (in our house, it seems to be adapters and power cords for cell phones). We have a box of them that we dip into every now and then when one of us leaves an adapter or power cord in a hotel room or somewhere else on our travels.

Other than that, my desk is also home to extras such as an external USB hub, a powered speaker system (I love to listen to music while I am working), several lamps, an external microphone, and a webcam for recording videos and conducting video conferences.

However, if you were to go through the drawers in my desk, you would find a whole lot more gadgetry, from mini-power strips that I use when I am traveling to external speakers for my laptop, external batteries for my cell phone, and a handheld video camera. You would also find a small radio-controlled helicopter—not exactly a business essential but something to use while I am thinking, or at least that is my excuse. The one other item (not a gadget, but one that you will find not only in and on my desk and other locations around the apartment but in the bags that I travel with) is a notebook. I am never without one.

The Out of Office worker based at home also has greater opportunity to furnish their office in a way that reflects their personality. Many organizations, especially those in the U.S. who have to comply with strict rules about workplace safety imposed by OSHA, have had employees remove items from cubicle and office space because of noncompliance. Items such as coffee makers, space heaters, and other electrical devices have gone. In addition, the need to use the space primarily for work often leaves cubicle workers with little room for self-expression.

The home-based Out of Office worker is less constrained and can, with only a few limitations, express themselves and their personality throughout their office.

Dayna Steele, keynote speaker and author, shared with me that she enjoys having a TV in her office:

I love, love working from home and having TV/CNN in my home office.

There are very few people who work in a cubicle that I would envisage being allowed to have a TV with them! Of course, for some businesses they are a workplace essential, but for the majority it would be seen as a distraction and an impediment to an efficient workplace.

Another of the conflicts that arises when organizations examine Out of Office working is that what works in the organizational environment probably won't work in the home setting, and vice versa.

The technology that people rely on to enable the Out of Office work style is as varied as the people themselves.

Dan Ramirez, a social media manager and publicist, relies on Google products to stay in touch wherever he is:

> *I have to say that Google has to be the best platform out there. With Gmail, Google docs, Google+, Calendar, and more, you can't go wrong. I'm able to automatically sync everything between my two computers and my phone. Google has made it possible for me to hold my office in my hand.*

I think that Dan has hit on a really important element of the way technology is enabling many more people to explore the option of Out of Office working: "to hold my office in my hand."

Beyond a few select futurists, who would have imagined two decades ago that holding all the devices that enabled people to do their job would be contained in one small device? If you think back to the information workers space as it first appeared, there was the computer or a terminal connected to one, a fax machine, a printer, a telephone, perhaps a voice recorder, maybe an answering machine or a message-taking service. In some offices, perhaps there was a radio or even a television to allow people to stay connected with current affairs via the news.

All of those devices or their replacements are now embodied in a phone or tablet that fits into a pocket or bag. In addition, there are more options available: Those devices can now be used for video conferencing, and they can be used as a camera that not only can take photos and video but also share them with as many people as the person using it wants to share them with.

Others find that a particular piece of hardware has become indispensable for them to be able to work Out of Office from the home or on the road.

Arthur Cooper, who runs Optimum 7, can't be without his iPad, not just for the sake of the gadget but because of what it enables him to achieve:

> *My iPad, with Wi-Fi and cellular enabled. I can use critical apps like LogMeIn to access my home/business network. FaceTime to chat with my wife and see her at the same time (I get the better of that deal). I also use it to browse the Web, read the news, weather, sports, entertainment, etc.*

The iPad is one tool that enables both work and pleasure; it is little wonder that working Out of Office is on the rise. Tools that enable individuals to be as effective at home or on the road as they were in the traditional office setting and at the same time provide ways for them to avoid boredom are providing individuals with choices about their workspace and work time.

Notice that among the benefits Arthur listed was the ability to stay in touch with his wife. Out of Office workers are likely to be more flexible in their approach to working hours, but they are equally more likely to want to be more connected to their personal lives.

The Employee Based at Home

For Out of Office working to be truly successful, an organization needs to understand this need and make tools, software, and time available for that to be achieved.

With the rise in popularity of "Bring Your Own Device" (the arrangement where businesses are allowing employees to connect to the company-owned infrastructure via their own phone, tablet, or computer instead of providing the employees with them) in many organizations, employees now expect that the device they are using for work can and will also be used for personal entertainment. This further blurs the lines of when someone is on work time and when they are on their own time.

If an organization expects their employee to answer emails on their device outside of normal office hours, can they, in all fairness, expect to control the use of the device for other activities?

For those who work from home for an organization and are supplied with equipment to enable them to do so, this is a tricky question. If your company provides your computer, without which you are unable to do your job, should you also use it for personal social media? I do know of individuals who maintain two computers in their home office: one supplied by their company and one for personal use. They feel that this is the only way in which they can adequately and appropriately divide their work life from their personal life and still retain a sense of freedom and personality in their online life.

Each organization handles this differently, mostly in ways that match the overall culture of the organization. Those that tend toward the more conservative, perhaps more controlling management style, will also tend toward imposing stricter controls on the use of employee-owned devices. I know of at least one organization that implemented strict rules governing the use of employee-owned devices for accessing business email, including the requirement that monitoring software be placed on the device and that an eight-digit password be implemented. Many of the employees simply declined to use their personal device any longer to access work emails, with of course the subsequent decline in productivity.

For those working Out of Office for an organization, that luxury is unrealistic; they cannot simply refuse to connect back to the parent organization because they own a device. It is more likely that they will seek to obtain a device from their organization, particularly a computer, rather than use their own. Again, this leaves the employee in the unenviable position of having to draw a distinct line between home and work while at the same time being in only one location: home.

Human resources, information technology, and line managers responsible for managing and supporting Out of Office workers face the challenge of providing an environment that is conducive to the efficient productivity of the employee while at the same time maintaining company policies regarding security of information and addressing other concerns that organizations of any size face when dealing with data.

There is no "one size fits all" solution, and as technology advances and enables increased connectivity from an increasing number of locations, organizations will need to find ways to adapt and meet this changing landscape of the workplace. Far from being a minor detour in the path of human work life, I really believe that Out of Office working is the direction that many roles will take in the near future.

Of course, not everyone agrees with this vision. Marisa Mayer, CEO of Yahoo!, raised eyebrows in 2013 by announcing that all Yahoo! employees would be required to work from the Yahoo! offices in San Francisco. Although this was seen by some as taking away a privilege, others saw it as a move to unify a fractured organization. However, the tech giant wasn't the only organization to make this move. Best Buy, the U.S.-based retail organization, terminated their flexible working arrangement after eight years, also in 2013. Both organizations have stated that their moves are not a comment on flexible working but rather moves that are right for their particular organizations.

It is difficult to make sound observations on these and other organizations that are moving away from the Out of Office work style without knowing the internal dynamics involved. Certainly it is true that some Out of Office workers, especially those based from home, abuse the situation to their own advantage. Mayer cited employees who had created start-ups from their homes on company time while working from home for Yahoo!.

That said, it is hard to imagine that the situation for Yahoo! or Best Buy was such widespread abuse that the issue couldn't be managed on an individual level rather than in broad brushstrokes that will leave many employees looking for a new position or at least feel that the company they work for is no longer supportive of them.

I am not implying that any organization that doesn't allow Out of Office working and in particular work-from-home scenarios is draconian. Every organization finds a way to motivate, manage, and retain employees differently. However, I do believe that this style of working is now becoming part of the consideration set for employees when choosing where to work. Just as employers are seeking greater flexibility from their employees, so too are employees seeking greater flexibility from their employers. As always, the conversation about working conditions has to be two-way and cannot be simply dictated by one side or the other.

The work-from-home discussion is being mirrored on many levels at corporations. Not the least of which is the access to social media sites. As I outlined earlier, if an employer wants an employee to be accessible via email outside of working hours, is it not a fair expectation that an employee might have access to personal Internet use during working hours.

Arguments flow back and forth around this point, with those against it citing productivity, security, breach of confidentiality, and so on. Of course, technology has made all of these arguments moot. There is nothing to stop an employee bringing an internet-connected device to work and using it at their desk; in fact, many already do in the form of their smartphones. So by blocking access on a company-owned computer, has the organization really achieved anything or have they simply moved the access to a more covert action?

This also speaks to the issue of trust. Does blocking access to certain websites convey a message that the organization lacks trust in its employees? Does it say that they don't feel they are mature enough to be allowed to blur the lines between personal and professional?

Equally, it can be argued that by allowing workshifting or telecommuting from home, an organization gains a more flexible employee, who, because they feel valued, will be more productive at a lower overall cost to the employer. Although the proponents of this work style rally around this argument, employers are not all convinced.

Just as with access to certain websites, the granting or denying of the ability to work from home can also be seen as relating to the level of trust an organization places in its employees. Does not granting the ability say more about how employees are viewed than it does about an organizations logistical ability to support the work style?

Without doubt an organization making Out of Office working an option is sending a message that they place a great deal of trust in their employees to conduct themselves as professionals—a message that, in most cases, will be met with a degree of professionalism that is hard to measure and to achieve in a purely in-office environment.

The truth is that change is hard, and at an organizational level, change can be extremely hard. Often, it is a long process of evolution rather than revolution. I don't believe that we have seen the last of the evolutionary steps at Yahoo!, Best Buy, and other organizations that have apparently recanted their belief in the work-from-home/Out of Office work style. Whatever organizational priorities have created the about-turn in their attitude are likely to be resolved, and I am certain we will see the reintroduction of some form of Out of Office work style from these companies in the future. Of course, just as those organizations are evolving, so too is the work style itself and the technology that enables it.

Although we are still a long way from the home of *The Jetsons* (an American cartoon from the 1960s that envisaged automated homes with robot assistants), the amount of domestic home automation that we are seeing being introduced will ultimately have an impact on the Out of Office worker based at home—from smartphone apps that control lighting, heating, entertainment, and other electronics in the home, to appliances that are connected to the Internet to enable them to interact with services independent of the owner. Devices that allow motion gesturing such as the Xbox Connect, developed by Microsoft initially for gaming purposes, are being adapted to have business applications. They also allow for video conferencing to take place away from a computer (rather they can take place as part of the whole home computer). Because these lines blur at an increasingly rapid pace, we will also see the lines between work and home life blur. When time and location become truly irrelevant and an individual can be a virtual presence at an office anywhere on the planet and is able to physically interact with objects (or at the very least interact with virtual objects) at the same time as their co-workers, the possibilities for Out of Office working become endless.

The evolution of the home and what that word means to individuals will have perhaps the greatest impact on those working from home. In many urban environments, the cost of housing has risen so sharply that cost per square foot means affordable accommodation is shared, and tends toward the functional rather than the futuristic, especially in the rental market.

For those living and working in these hubs, the choice to work from home is unrealistic; they can, however, work Out of Office in other locations, so perhaps we will see a divide in the Out of Office work style where those who live in areas that have affordable accommodations that provide sufficient space to realistically entertain working from home will do so, and others will find and create new working environments, ones that we have only barely begun to consider.

5

Working on the Road

Working from the road presents a different set of challenges than those presented when working from home. The most obvious is, of course, the lack of familiarity with the surroundings, which in itself can be a big barrier to productivity.

Broadly speaking, there are two main categories of Out of Office workers who travel: those who experience this work style regularly and those who experience it infrequently. Both groups face similar challenges, but some additional challenges are experienced by those who are not regularly on the road. For them, the unfamiliar surroundings, the lack of access to equipment and accessories, and the overall disconnect with their usual routine can all form challenges that distract from being productive. For others, a chance to break the usual routine and work from different surroundings can actually encourage them to be more productive. Regardless of which group the Out of Office worker finds themselves in, they will face some challenges they are not used to.

Essentials Items

Whatever the reason the Out of Office worker finds themselves on the road, maintaining productivity is essential. To this end, most choose to travel with a device that enables them to continue to produce work, stay connected via email, the Web, and in some cases video, and allow for some entertainment. Whether this device is simply a smartphone, a tablet, a laptop, or a combination of these, the one thing they all have in common is the need for power.

There is nothing more frustrating than leaving home without a power cord for your device. Why do you think there are so many vendors at airports selling them, often at greatly inflated prices? They know you have to have power, they know you need it now, so, within reason, you are willing to pay whatever they ask.

How many phone chargers, cables, or external battery packs are sold at airports around the world every day? Southwest Airlines, a carrier based in the United States, reports finding more than 10,000 items a month left behind on their planes. That is just one carrier and just one country.

Leaving an essential piece of equipment at home is bad enough, but leaving it on the plane can be even worse. If the item is a power cord, it is fairly easy to replace, but leaving a phone, tablet, or laptop behind could be catastrophic.

If nothing else, the loss of a device leads to delays in travel and hampers the individual's ability to remain in contact. Of course, there are pay phones in airports, but how many of us actually remember phone numbers these days? If you had to phone a client or even your business office without the contact book in your phone, would you be able to?

Leaving a computer behind could severely affect a small business owner or solopreneur, especially if they don't back up the data stored on it regularly. A global survey conducted by EVault in 2012 found that 22 percent of employees had company data stored on one more personal devices, but 78 percent of businesses didn't have a mobile data recovery plan in place.

That is a lot of sensitive, potentially damaging, and at the very least operationally significant information that could be lost, stolen, or misappropriated. For a solopreneur, the loss could signal the end of their business, if the data on the lost device included customer contact information, work in progress, and other business-critical information. Replacing the device might be out of their immediate financial reach, so they are in effect paralyzed.

The nightmare of losing all of my business data is one reason why I still use a desktop computer and cloud backup services such as Dropbox. If I lose my laptop, there would be financial implications and of course a huge nuisance factor, but there is nothing on it that isn't also stored in two other places, and provided I replace the device, there's nothing that can't be accessed again quickly. The same goes for my phone, which is backed up regularly so that I don't lose my contact information.

These are simple steps, and although there are costs associated with them, these costs are worth paying given that the potential loss could be the entire business.

Having reached a destination, finding locations to work can be an intimidating (or at least very frustrating) experience. When in your own neighborhood, you acquire a certain familiarity with the places that provide you with the right facilities for working in. Whether those are coffee shops, hotels, cafes, or bookstores, when you are traveling, especially to somewhere you are unfamiliar with, finding those comfortable spots to work and be productive from can be a challenge.

In major cities in the U.S., it is fairly easy to find locations of chain brands such as Starbucks. In fact, I am convinced that part of their popularity is the familiarity that they provide travelers with. The Marriott Hotel chain has this built in to their branding. All the hotels look the same and the hotel-provided equipment such as ironing boards and irons are always in the same place. Doing this means that Marriott can offer a repeatable experience to their guests, and their guests have one less thing to think about while they are traveling.

Even traveling overseas this is true. I have often resorted to U.S. chain restaurants when traveling in Asia and Europe simply because I have some level of expectation of what I will find on the menu, and I don't have to think too hard about what I am going to eat. That might seem slightly xenophobic, but it is more about comfort than not wanting to experience the local cuisine—which I often do. After being on a plane for 14 hours, trying to figure out what to eat is the last thing I want to do.

These familiar signposts are a boon to the infrequent traveler. Knowing that a particular chain provides free Wi-Fi, a certain meal or beverage, a type of bed, or even a particular favorite sandwich gives them an oasis-type appeal that cannot be overstated. It is precisely for that reason the infrequent traveler can be best advised to seek them out when on a trip. Unless the trip is for pleasure, you have more than enough to think about in terms of conducting the business you are traveling for, so why stress yourself out trying to find a good restaurant, hotel, or free Wi-Fi. Go with what you know so you can get the job done and relax.

Perhaps the most basic of requirements when traveling is access to funds. Whether traveling domestically or overseas, you have to be able to pay for your hotel, cabs or a rental car, meals, and everything else. Although cash might have been king once, only the most questionable of hotels accepts cash these days. Everything is plastic and must be backed up with a photo ID. So what happens when you are traveling and suddenly find that the funds you thought you had access to aren't available?

Jacque Miller, a clinical outreach specialist with Sober Living, had just that experience:

> I had traveled to Prescott, Arizona to call on a number of clients and had checked into my hotel the evening before, got up, went to a couple of appts, and decided to grab a bite to eat before going to my next appt. I ran into In & Out Burger to grab a cheeseburger and drink, and when they swiped the card it was declined. I had them try it again, thinking

surely it was a mistake. It was declined again and so I paid cash, ate, and left. I did not have my personal debit or credit card with me and my big concern was that when I checked out from the hotel I would not have any money to pay for it. I called the credit card company and they said my card had been comprised and that it was blocked and they would not unblock it but they would send me a new card in 7–10 days.

Of course that wasn't going to help me much. Luckily the hotel had already run the charges when I checked in, and I was only in town for one more day, so I made it with what cash I had on me. So it all worked out.

I was traveling with my boss and the same thing happened to his credit card, and I ended up having to put all of his travel expenses on my card and, of course, that meant it all went on my expense account too.

An incident like this is hard to plan for. Jacque managed to work around it, but what if the hotel hadn't run the charges? What if she were facing other expenses? How do you work around that type of situation?

I have found myself in a very similar situation, away from home, funds unavailable, for exactly the same reason as Jacque. My solution was to phone home and to have money sent by wire transfer via Western Union. The fees were minimal and the transfer only took a few hours. I was then able to pay the cash onto a personal card and cover my expenses that way.

The key to these situations is to not panic, which is of course easier said than done when you find yourself in a strange city, without access to money, and you have no personal contacts locally. Whether it's not having access to funds or finding that your time is swallowed up in ways you hadn't imagined, when you arrive at your destination there is always a solution or at the very least an amusing story to be gained from the experience.

Robert Pearce, CTO of Rideshare, tells a very funny story of deciding to work on vacation while his family went out to dinner:

Throughout my European trip, I had struggled with finding a balance between time spent working versus time spent enjoying the scenery. I would try to wake up early to work, work while in the car/train, and work in the evenings. However, as everyone with their own business knows, work schedules tend to fly out the window and are replaced with around-the-clock work hours. The best decision I made was during a gorgeous evening in Radda in Chianti (Chianti region), Italy. I had decided that I had not accomplished much during this day and was going to have to stay in for the evening while my family went to dinner. What "type" of dinner they were attending was something else entirely.

I was aroused from my mid-work somnambulism by the sound of drumming. There were the drums at first, but these were soon followed by shouts, the clang of metal on metal, and knights in armor passing my window. You know that moment where you are convinced you've slipped through a crack in time and have travelled to another era? My curiosity more than aroused, I threw the windows wide open and bore witness to a gang of jesters, hawkers, owlers (like hawkers, but with owls), swordsmen, knights, and musicians. I left my computer behind (I had just travelled through time, obviously; work no longer mattered) and followed this parade of Italian antiquity through the streets until we came upon the town's centre square, which was populated by tables full of people, jars of wine, platters of food, and, of course, my family. The dinner which they were attending turned out to be the 500th anniversary of a victorious battle with a neighboring town, and all locals and visitors were invited to the festivities.

We drank, enjoyed the festivities, learned Italian curse words, and made many friends. Never have I ever been so thankful to be swept through time.

Not exactly a common experience, but one of the things you will learn about working from the road is to never underestimate the potential for a seemingly ordinary journey to turn into something quite different and very distracting.

Carolyn Pearson, Founder of Maiden Voyage, a UK-based global network for women travelers, shared a very different experience with me, but before sharing the story I also want to share how traveling and working from the road led to a whole new career for Carolyn and how she was inspired to found Maiden Voyage.

At the time, Carolyn worked for Independent Television (ITV), a British television production company. They were looking for a new software vendor, and so she traveled to Los Angeles to meet with some prospective providers. Because her meetings were at the beginning of the week, she decided to travel early and experience Los Angeles over the weekend prior to the meetings. She enjoys traveling so the thought of being a tourist for a couple of days was very appealing. She had booked her hotel next door to the software vendor's offices, in downtown Los Angeles. Like many large cities, the business district was deserted on Friday night and for the weekend.

While she managed to catch a cab and see some of the more interesting parts of Los Angeles, each evening she was restricted to her hotel and their offerings for food. In her words:

> *Friday night and Saturday night I was stuck in the hotel, eating hotel food, with just a couple of business men hanging around. It was just really boring. I thought, "My God, if there had been another woman that I could have met up with, you know, and gone off and done something with, it would have been fantastic."*

The experience got Carolyn thinking: She talked the idea through with a few contacts and when she got positive feedback on the idea she decided to put together a prototype of what would become Maiden Voyage. Having put the prototype together, she found a software company willing to develop the actual site.

It was hardly on the Web any time at all before a magazine contacted her and wanted to run a feature article on her new network. From that article, *The New York Times* included it in a feature that led to a TV interview with CNN. That triggered a global response from women travelers.

One of Carolyn's early decisions about the network was that she would call everyone who signed up for the service to make sure they were in fact a woman. This turned out to be a challenging decision once the network took off. Carolyn found herself calling Uganda, Ethiopia, Kazakhstan, Yemen, Japan, United States, and other countries, all from her kitchen.

After five years, it has grown into a full-time job that includes offering training courses to hotels on how to better adapt their offerings to women guests. The site offers advice, guidance, and networking opportunities to women travelers and is growing rapidly. All of this grown from Carolyn's experiences as a woman traveler who wanted to get more from her trips.

Oh, and Carolyn's story from the road?

> *I was staying in London, the day before my interview with CNN, and so I contacted the concierge in the hotel and asked if they could organize someone to give me a blow dry the next morning. I just trusted that he would find a proper hairdresser.*
>
> *The hotel had upgraded me to their penthouse, which was on its own floor with no other rooms around. I got up the next morning and there was a knock on my door. When I opened it, there was a Rastafarian guy with a sports bag. I thought, "Should I be really letting this guy in, he could have a hammer or anything in that bag."*

Anyway, he started to dry my hair and I thought I would quiz him on his hairdressing. He didn't seem very comfortable with hair, which worried me. I asked him where he had been working recently and he replied, "Oh, I've been away for a while," so then I thought he's been in prison!

He took 40 minutes to dry my hair and it turned out looking like straw. I had no time to do anything about it and had to go to the studio and do the interview with CNN with my hair looking like that. To top it all off he charged me 90 pounds (approx. U.S. $150).

Definitely a tale of caution: Relying on hotel concierge services doesn't always pay off. Being a woman traveling alone brings its own set of hazards—certainly more so than men traveling alone. Maiden Voyage hopes to provide education for women, among other things, to assist women in getting the best possible experience from their travels.

Carolyn's story shows that even the most experienced travelers can run into situations that they were not prepared for, but again really shows that just rolling with the situation is often the best way (if not the only way) to cope.

Smartphones and Smart Travelers

Finding ideal places to work, eat and stay while away from home has become increasingly easy. No longer are you reliant on the local knowledge of a taxi driver who picks you up at the airport. Applications for smartphones that provide local information are plentiful. From rating and review services such as Yelp to social apps such as Foursquare, shown in Figure 5.1, these tools allow even the novice traveler to navigate an unfamiliar city with the ease of a master.

In this figure, you can see how the smartphone application Foursquare provides recommendations for places to eat near your current location. These happen to be recommendations for places near my home, and included in the recommendations is a list of my friends who use that app that have been to those locations. This additional information can greatly assist the traveler visiting a new city. If people you know have been there and you like similar things, then maybe the place is going to provide you with a good experience, even if you aren't familiar with it.

The smartphone is also providing travelers with alternatives to basic services such as cabs. Services such as Uber provide travelers with private cars with a driver (see Figure 5.2). Of course, these can be more expensive than traditional cabs, but the experience is of a much higher quality, and when the streets seem deserted of cabs, the Uber service is an extremely reliable alternative.

Figure 5.1 *Foursquare.*

Figure 5.2 *Uber.*

Uber uses the GPS location of your phone to pinpoint where you are, allowing you to select a point on the map that you want to be picked up at. It can be your current location or another location. You can also tell the service when you need the car and, of course, your destination. Although only available in major cities at the moment, the list of cities the service operates in is growing rapidly. Now, rather than standing on a sidewalk competing with other travelers for a cab, you can remain comfortably sitting in a coffee shop, bar, restaurant, or your hotel and simply order up your car. As they say, it's the little things. In fact, making life easier while on the road is something that the smartphone excels at.

Airline apps allow you to check in before you arrive at the airport, select your seat, and generate your boarding card so that you no longer need the paper version (you simply scan your phone at the gate). They can also provide updates to your flight status and advise you of gate changes and delays.

In fact, it is hard to think of another device that has changed the travel experience more than the smartphone. Not only is it used to keep the owner connected to their business world, it makes light work of previously onerous tasks and can be used for entertainment and for staying in touch with home and office via video. Some people have even been known to use it for making phone calls!

Other smartphone applications allow you to perform tasks such as scanning business cards directly into your contacts, scan receipts so that they can be added to expense reports, edit documents, and access cloud-based storage.

I have used my smartphone to view, edit, and sign and send contracts for new business while waiting for a plane at the airport, something that I would have previously had to wait until I returned to my office to do. Being faster, more responsive, and more organized has a very positive impact on relationships with clients and co-workers alike.

Of course, the entertainment aspect of the smartphone shouldn't be overlooked either. Whether playing games, watching movies or TV shows, or reading a book, the traveler is offered a myriad of entertainment possibilities. No longer is the traveler limited to whatever entertainment they can find at their destination: They can now take their own entertainment with them. Some applications even allow you to access your DVR at home and watch shows you have recorded there from your smartphone or tablet.

One more feature of the smartphone that is indispensable and that gives it a distinct advantage over being present in an office is the off switch. Whether forced to turn it off during takeoff and landing, or simply choosing to turn it off for some self-imposed quiet time, the ability to control when you are available is perhaps one of the biggest luxuries of working from the road.

Staying Healthy

Traveling away from home for some means having to skip visits to the gym, running with a buddy, or a workout with a group of friends; in fact, staying on plan is one of the biggest challenges mentioned to me when I asked people about their lives on the road.

Eating healthily or at the very least not abandoning good eating completely was a challenge also mentioned by many. From pretzels on the plane to dessert in the hotel room, or even just the vending machine in the hallway, the temptations for the traveler are seemingly endless.

When I first started to travel on business, I found myself like a kid in a candy store. The meals, the endless possibilities for indulgence seemed just too good to be true. Of course, in a way they were. Although my company footed the bill for my meals, my body soon started to foot the bill for my indulgence.

A lot of hotels provide in-house gyms, so it would seem the excuse not to work out is removed; of course, if you are flying to a location in this era of checked baggage fees, many people opt to only take carry-on, which comes with the challenge of packing only the essentials. That pair of running shoes and a set or two of workout gear can only be packed at the cost of other clothing items. So the excuse remains, "I'd workout but I don't have room for my gear."

In reality, there are many ways it is possible to maintain a workout schedule while on the road without having to pack additional clothing. Websites such as Nerd Fitness (www.nerdfitness.com), Body Ripped (www.bodyripped.net), and various other online publications from *The New York Times*, *Men's Health*, and *Real Simple*, to *Shape* and *Self* offer hotel room workouts using nothing but your own body weight. Don't forget YouTube either. Workout videos aimed specifically at the traveler staying in a hotel abound there. So the only equipment you need is the furniture in your room and the only workout gear you need to wear is your underwear. Problem solved.

For those who feel the need for workout equipment but don't have the time to hit the gym in the hotel or don't have access to one, equipment from companies such as TRX Training (www.trxtraining.com) allow you to take the gym with you. Providing a low profile for easy packing, this type of equipment is best used under instruction as a beginner, but once the basics are learned it can be used anywhere that has a door and some floor space (I wouldn't recommend trying it in the airplane bathroom, though!).

The smallest workout equipment that you can carry is probably a workout DVD, from P90X to TV tie-ins such as *The Biggest Loser*, the type, style, and intensity of workouts available on DVD are almost bewildering. I can't imagine there not being a workout DVD that fits your style, and after all you are probably carrying a device with you that is capable of video playback, even if you have to transfer the contents of the DVD to it. Have you run out of excuses yet?

That really is what we provide ourselves—excuses. We might frame them as obstacles, but really they are excuses. This comes back to the core essentials of the type of personality that is best suited to the Out of Office work style—one of which is undoubtedly self-discipline. If you can find reasons not to look after your health, you are likely to be able to find excuses not to complete other tasks. This has nothing to do with being lazy or being a slacker. This is more about not having the level of self-awareness and self-monitoring to recognize those moments when you are making choices that aren't going to result in the best of outcomes.

Eating while on the road can present more of a challenge for those with particular dietary needs. Donna Ledbetter shared her experiences of trying to find vegan food while traveling:

> *I was on travel for a conference in Colorado and got violently ill. I am vegan and had very few food choices available. I believe that eating the same food day in and day out was what caused me stomach trouble. In the end, I wound up spending a lot of my own money throughout the week getting cabs to and from restaurants with food I could eat. After that experience, I vowed to do what I could to help other people like me not to have to endure getting sick like I did because of limited food choices. So I started a travel website and podcast focused on travel for vegans. Working on the road inspired me to start a new business. It's just getting off the ground (no pun intended), but more people are finding useful information about vegan travel every day.*

Like Carolyn, Donna's experiences have led not only to her having a better coping strategy while on the road, she has created a business from it, which definitely indicates that there is both a lot to be gained from working from the road and that many of us have shared experiences that we can all learn from.

I avoid gluten in my diet as well as carbonated drinks of any kind. This isn't particularly difficult to do when traveling, but when I first moved to that way of eating I would often forget and order a diet coke or similar beverage because I was in a strange place, perhaps eating out with clients, and that was what everyone else was ordering, so it just seemed natural. Part of the problem with staying healthy on the road is the sense of dislocation: What comes naturally at home can be easily forgotten in the midst of finding your way around a strange town or when distracted by other people.

It is all part of the challenge of the Out of Office work style faced by those working away from familiar surroundings. Even if it is a location that you travel to regularly, it still isn't home. For some that is actually a bonus, giving them much needed time away from the normal routine and providing the opportunity for fresh perspectives, but for many others it is disconcerting and a distraction that can lead to broken habits and comfort eating (raises hand guiltily). It can take a conscious effort to ensure that the distractions are kept to a minimum, just as they are at home, although the distractions when traveling can involve a whole different set of distractions than those provided at home.

Getting Rewards

Travel is the only thing that you buy and leaves you richer.

—Unknown

The rewards for traveling for business come in many forms: the tangible and the intangible, from hotel and airline reward programs to new experiences. The business traveler is a type of worker that has a set of rewards available to them that is incomparable to other types of workers.

I don't travel frequently enough with the same carrier to earn sufficient miles to get any real rewards. I tend to buy the best ticket that gets me to my destination. However, I recently traveled with my girlfriend, who travels globally and frequently and has achieved the top status with her airline of choice. From the express security lane at the airport to the use of the plush lounge and the upgraded seats, the whole experience was definitely better and it cost her nothing other than loyalty to one specific brand.

The same was true when we reached our destination. She has a similar status with a hotel chain: We got a room on a higher floor, access to a concierge lounge with free breakfast and beverages, free newspapers, and more.

All of this added to the enjoyment of the trip. For those who travel frequently, these are just some of the benefits they realize.

Of course, airlines also offer free flights to their loyal customers in return for "cashing in" the points they have earned, and hotels offer free nights. It has been noted that lately these are becoming harder to achieve as both airlines and hotels have started to increase the number of points required to achieve these types of rewards. "No such thing as a free lunch" comes rapidly to mind when I read stories of how much the cost of these "free" rewards has increased, placing them out of the reach of all but the most frequent of travelers. That said, it is still a reward worth having, and if your business sees you traveling a lot, you are probably looking for any and all rewards.

Most business travelers I know tell me the same thing: It sounds glamorous to be visiting lots of different cities, whether domestically or internationally, but often that means they only see the airport, the inside of a taxi or rental car, and their hotel room. If they manage half a day in their destination city, they consider themselves lucky—and of course the travel takes them away from home and in many cases loved ones. A free hotel room doesn't seem much of a reward when balanced against that for many people.

The ultimate reward for business travelers is perhaps the odd occasion when they can have a family member or friend travel with them. Some companies frown upon this, whereas others embrace it, provided that it is accounted for in the right way.

I'm lucky that my girlfriend's company falls into the second category. They have no problem with me tagging along on her trips as long as I pay my own airfare and food costs. Although we don't get much time together on these trips—she is there to work after all—I get to see great places and we are at least together at night, which makes the trip better for her and for me.

When negotiating salary and benefits with a company, elements like this are often overlooked by employees. I would say that these types of benefits can easily make up for not realizing the salary figure you were looking for.

A company I worked for actually paid for one vacation a year for each member of the senior management team. This was to encourage them to take their vacation days and to come back recharged and energized. It was a generous benefit and something that definitely added to employee loyalty as well as achieving the goal of ensuring that the executives actually took time off.

It is important to look for rewards from sources outside of just the travel and tourism industry. Of course, we are used to them offering rewards, but many other service providers also offer travelers rewards. Hotels often have agreements with local businesses to offer guests discounts on services, and local restaurants will often offer discounted meals on weekdays during the early evening.

If you can be flexible with your schedule, it is possible to get rewarded for your travel from a variety of places that you might not have thought of. If you are going to have some free time in your destination city, it is worth researching what attractions might interest you and what discounts are offered for visitors. Places such as New York City, for example, have many discounted offers for the attractions there, whether using the New York CityPASS or one of the various coupon books, it's possible to find a deal on many of the tourist destinations in the city.

Websites such as Restaurant.com offer discounted meals at restaurants in major cities across the United States. Although your company will probably be paying the bill for your meals, who doesn't like earning a reward or two? And saving the company some money can only look good on your expense report.

The traveling Out of Office worker has a series of hurdles to negotiate to achieve the same level of productivity as their in-office counterparts: They also have opportunities that aren't presented to their counterparts in the same way.

Technology allows us to communicate with a range of people that was unthinkable just a few decades ago, but for all of the video conferencing, email, and social networks, most business people I speak to agree that meeting someone face-to-face is the most rewarding and the method that most often leads to new business, additional business, or just the cementing of existing relationships.

Those traveling Out of Office workers might seem to have a great life, and as we have seen in this chapter there are definitely some benefits and rewards to their travels. They also perform a function that is hard to replicate from within the bounds of an office environment. With the packed schedules that everyone in business operates on, having a customer come to your office for a meeting is not only impractical in many cases, in most it is just not something that can happen.

When I was traveling for a previous company, we were pitching for a huge new contract. At the time the company was small and relatively unheard of, and we were up against some very big names in the industry. However, what separated us from the other bidders was that the CEO, CTO, and myself all attended the pitch meeting in person. We had traveled from across the globe to attend the meeting. None of the other companies sent representatives, choosing instead to make their pitches via teleconferencing, video-conferencing, or other technology-based presentation methods.

We got the business. I was informed later that one of the deciding factors was that the executives making the decision were convinced because we were in the room with them, they were able to look us in the eye and shake our hands.

Sometimes, for all our technology and advances in communication, it comes down to a solid handshake and meeting a person eye-to-eye to convince them to do business.

6

Getting Organized

Being an Out of Office worker requires as much if not more organization than the in-office counterpart. The in-office worker benefits from having support networks within the larger organization. In many larger organizations, administrative tasks are carried out by specialized staff. Even in mid-sized organizations, it is not uncommon to have someone whose designation is usually something akin to Office Manager. Their role is to ensure that the items necessary for the operation of the office environment are provided. From paperclips to plumbing and beyond, the Office Manager and their team (if they have one) are the people to which other employees turn when they need items to support their role.

When you work from home, that immediate support network is missing. When you run out of staples, there is no stationery cupboard to turn to. If the A/C breaks down in the middle of summer, there isn't a maintenance crew on hand to be called out to fix it. Even the trash can in your office doesn't magically empty itself over night for you.

All of these things and many more that the average in-office worker takes for granted are suddenly your responsibility. When a friend left a large consultancy to start working for themselves from home, their first comment on the first day they started the business was, "Where is the intern to get my coffee? Oh that's right, I'm that intern and everybody else now!"

Although there is a lot to be said for working from home, as I have already outlined in previous chapters, the key, at least in my opinion, to making it a successful situation is to be organized—extremely organized. That isn't something that comes naturally to some people, myself included, and it should certainly be a consideration when contemplating making the move to Out of Office working. That is not to say that the level of organization has to be at the obsessive level, but knowing where everything is, where it needs to be, and how to find it just makes life a whole lot easier than the alternative.

If you haven't transitioned to Out of Office working yet and you work for an organization, take a look around your office the next time you are there. Think about all the things that are in your office or cube. I don't mean just the desk and chair; think about the other elements that make up your office environment. Lighting, heating, carpeting, office supplies, janitorial supplies, printers, fax machines (some people still use them!), photocopiers, security services, on-site gym, on-site nurse, cafeteria, and, yes, the desk and chair you use.

All of those things are going to be supplied by you when you start Out of Office working. Whether from home, on the road, or a combination of both, you are going to have to manage all of those elements that are simply a given in the office.

Now you might say, "Well, I already have an office at home or a space that can become one and it already has heat and light and flooring. I have an all-in-one printer that can be a fax and copier. My kitchen is just down the hall so I don't need a cafeteria, and the cabinet under the kitchen sink always has cleaning supplies if I need to use them."

Okay, sounds like you have all your bases covered—or do you? When making the transition to Out of Office working, are you going to include a "maintenance fee" per month that will be paid to cover the extras? Can you expense them or do you just have to accept those costs as part of the advantage of working Out of Office?

Are these expenses really that high? Paperclips don't cost much, nor does printer ink and printer paper. Screen wipes are pretty cheap, too. Very true, but now start to add them up. Over the total of a year, those items and many more can actually come to a decent amount. If you don't have an agreement in advance of making the transition, you could well end up having to just absorb the costs.

Of course, you might be able to write them off as an unreimbursed business expense (talk to an accountant about that), but I recommend thinking it through before you make the transition. Oh, and those cleaning supplies that live under the sink in the kitchen, those belong to the house not your office, so depending on how often you think you are going to clean your office, you might want to find a drawer in your desk to keep your own supplies.

Now, of course, at first reading this seems all very petty. You are going to be doing serious business working Out of Office. You don't need to concern yourself with paperclips and screen cleaners. After all, if your company trusts you to work unsupervised, surely you are mature enough to look after an office space. Therein lies the downfall of many an Out of Office worker. Taking for granted the little things that actually make the cogs of industry turn. If an army marches on its stomach, then business moves on stationery. Sound like an outrageous claim? Just think of the number of times that you have opened a desk drawer and not found at least a few items of stationery. Even though many people will talk about being fully digital, using only email, efax, video conferencing, and social media, the rest of the world is not yet paperless.

I'm sure we have all experienced the frustration of finding the only stapler that is near at hand empty of staples and having to track down the one person who keeps a supply of them in their desk. That frustration, when it happens alone can be something that contributes to the stress felt when working Out of Office. Having gone through that type of stress, along with other work-related stress, I've found that actually having a place for everything and everything in its place makes my life a lot easier and more enjoyable. As they say, it's the little things.

Working alone from home doesn't exempt you from this type of stress. All those additional items can be written off as a business expense, especially if you can show you are buying them solely for use in your home office (again, check with your accountant for exactly how much you can write off). Part of this organizational challenge is separating home from office, even though they occupy the same physical space.

There is much more to being organized than just staples, of course. However, according to organizational specialists, starting with the small things leads to a greater sense of organization. Along with basic organization, the experts also recommend regular cleaning of your office space, something that sounds obvious and, of course, happens for you when you work in-office. Now, I am far from a clean freak—as my girlfriend will testify—but even I see the benefit of a clean and orderly workspace.

I clean my office on a regular basis (or at least what I consider a regular basis) of all the accumulated detritus. This means taking all the piles of paper, assorted conference badges, sticky notes, notebook pages, notebooks, electronic devices, and other things off of the desk and putting them in piles on the floor of my office.

Having separated these items into their appropriate piles, it is time to make the hard decision—what stays and what goes? Now, it may be true that I am a bit of a hoarder. I have a tendency to hold on to things "just in case." At the age of 30, I pulled out an old favorite jacket from a storage box from when I was a teenager.

In the pocket was a shopping list that my mother had given me when I was 12. I'd kept it "just in case." Of course I threw it away, but now regret doing so, since my mother is no longer with us.

Of course, attaching sentimental images to office supplies is a bit of a stretch and more likely to indicate a propensity to hoarding than a true emotional attachment to that sticky note. Still, setting a shelf-life on the items on your desk (or in your closet) makes the decision a lot easier. If you haven't used, read, or referred to an item in a given period of time (a week, month, year, or decade, depending on how big your desk is), then it is time that item was retired. Now that might not mean actually trashing it, but rather filing it. As I mentioned in Chapter 2, "The Benefits," I have a desk previously used by a lawyer. It has large drawers on both sides that are perfect for filing, and I also use a separate two-drawer file cabinet to keep things ordered.

It can be surprising how often I have to refer back to past contracts, invoices, or proposals. Although all these things are also filed electronically, having a paper trail (literally) has proven more than once to be a useful practice.

One item that can become a clutter point is business cards. I used to collect them as though the greater number of them I had, the more successful I would be. So over the space of a few years, I ended up with hundreds of them. They were in drawers, file boxes, bags, suit pockets, special folders designed just to hold them— they were pervasive. After a few years of this, I suddenly realized that if I hadn't contacted the person, done business with them, or referred someone to them in the past 12 months, I probably never would. It was time to thin the collection.

Being a public speaker, it is not uncommon for people to come up to me at the end of a presentation and give me a business card. I'm not really sure the point of this: I mean, I understand that the person would like for a speaker to remember them, but given that I probably get handed 30 or so cards at any one event, it becomes impossible to remember everyone who simply hands me a card and runs away. I am a proponent of only exchanging business cards with people I know or at least have a strong suspicion I am going to want to follow up with in some manner— whether that is to do business with, to refer someone to them, or to have them refer me to someone.

If you truly don't see that type of connection, why trade cards? I usually carry very few business cards with me to events; that way, I am already restricting myself to only trading cards with people who meet my criteria. I'm sure some people will find this almost anti-social—after all, how much do business cards really cost? Isn't it just polite to trade cards with people at an event? Although I can see the basis of this argument, my thoughts are more along the lines of, is it really polite to just clutter their desk with one more business card they are never going to use?

I used to scan the business cards I received religiously: I thought that would make things more ordered and, of course, I would keep the actual card as a paper backup in case I lost my data somehow. As I mentioned earlier, I back up data to at least two different places, so, excluding the fall of mankind, it is extremely unlikely I will lose my data—I was already building redundancy into a system that had a surfeit of redundancy. I, of course, found ways to rationalize this, mostly with the "you never know" justification—which really just meant that I couldn't come up with a good reason for keeping them but wasn't sure I could just throw them away.

In the end, I came up with the same rule for business cards as I did for everything else: If I hadn't had contact with the person in the 12 months since I received their card, it was time to discard it, both physically and electronically. Let's face it: Our electronic devices can be just as cluttered as our physical spaces (more on that later in this chapter).

For those of you who want to store business cards, I highly recommend doing it electronically; there are so many devices and smartphone apps that make this easy, I find it hard to understand why anyone would not store them this way.

One such app I have used for quite some time is CamCard (see Figure 6.1). It utilizes the camera and optical character recognition (OCR) software to extract the information from the card and store it in your phone's contact database. It also supports you adding pictures and notes to the card so that you can store information about the person who gave you the card.

Figure 6.1   *CamCard.*

Having scanned a card, it will transfer the data to your contact database. I find this extremely useful as I sync my contacts with my computer; that way, I have the same data in at least two places and therefore I can email a contact from my phone or computer without having to actually look their email address up each time. I have to admit, I have never added a photo of someone who handed me a business card. That seems a little bit too invasive to me, but I am sure for some people it is a useful feature.

Having scanned the card and then added your notes and perhaps even a picture, you can throw the card away! Or better yet, give it back to the original owner. That's one less card that they have to replace. Eventually, they will be able to stop ordering new cards.

Having captured contact information from business cards and stored it, how do you now manage it and all the other contact information that you have on your device. Stop and think about that for a moment, you have contact information from social networks like Facebook, Twitter, LinkedIn, and any number of other networks, you have information that you have entered manually, from your email and a variety of other sources. Do you know where it is? Do you know how to quickly call up that information? Can you only do it by looking up someone's name? If you are like me, just when you really need someone's email address is the moment that you will completely blank on their name, or at least part of it, either first name or last name. This kind of thing happens all the time to me. I can remember exactly what someone looks like, I can remember the last conversation we had but I cannot for the life of me remember their name.

This is where contact management software or apps come to the rescue. Standard Contact address books on most phones are organized by name, either by first name or last name, and that is about it. On some devices you can search on fields such as company but on many you are stuck with just name. For people like me who think of their contacts in different ways, apps like Brewster (iPhone only) are a great addition to keeping you organized (see Figure 6.2).

Brewster organizes your contacts by name but also allows you to search in many different ways: visually—it produces pictures of your contacts taken from their social network profiles, by interest (for example if you have a contact from a kickball league that you are in then you can search by "kickball"), or by location—know where your contact lives, search for them that way. It also organizes your contacts based on the relationship you have with them—something I find very useful. For example, if I want to email my girlfriend, I don't want to have to search for her through my contact book. I want my device to know that she and I have a close relationship—Brewster handles that, managing your contacts based on the frequency you communicate with them, including via social networks (if you connect them to the app).

Figure 6.2 *Brewster.*

One more benefit from Brewster—it will send you reminders if you have been neglecting a previously much contacted connection, so it even helps you manage your social life.

As good as card scanners and OCR readers have become, there are always those "artsy" business cards that just can't be read, or are read incorrectly. On more than one occasion, I have used one of these apps only to find someone's name replaced by their company name, their phone number replaced with a fax number, and only a partial email address.

Still, for all their faults, applications and software that allow you to store your information electronically are definitely going to help cut down on the physical clutter in your office. However, much clutter you rid yourself of in the physical world I can guarantee you have replaced most (if not all of) it electronically.

I was reading an article recently on camera apps. The person who wrote the article claimed to have over 800 camera apps on their phone! Now that might have been an exaggeration to make a point, but even if it was a gross overestimate, that is an awful lot of data to have collected on one device. How many apps do you have on your phone? How many software programs do you have on your computer? How many of them do you use regularly? Just as with the physical items on your desk, this electronic clutter makes you less efficient. Those apps and programs slow your device down, which in turn slows you down. Having a contact database with thousands of names, telephone numbers, and email addresses might be impressive, but is it necessary? Think about how much faster your devices would operate if you cleaned out the clutter on the same basis as you cleaned out your physical workspace.

If you really feel you absolutely must retain every last piece of electronic data that you have acquired, then why not simply archive it to a cloud service. My preference is Dropbox, but there many to choose from. These services can be used simply as an additional hard drive, or you can schedule things to be moved to them (think of it as a maid service cleaning your physical space!). However you choose to use a remote storage service, it does provide a great way to clear clutter from your devices and free up both space and distractions while you are working.

Having done this once, I guarantee you will be surprised at how little you miss those items you have moved off your device. Then you will want to take a second look and see what else you haven't used in a while and clear even more from your devices. It can be quite a liberating experience, and unlike items in the physical world, unless you delete them, they are always somewhere that they can be restored to your device should you need the data.

Workflow

Although most office-based workers, whether Out of Office or in-office, would reject the notion that they have a lot in common with assembly-line workers, the principle of the assembly line has a lot of merit when organizing a workspace.

Having the items you use most nearest to the point of work and the items you use least furthest away makes for a much more organized and efficient space than some of the more, what might generously be referred to as "eclectic" workspaces. Part of that workflow is the layout of the room itself. In most corporate settings, this is actually undertaken by professional planners. This is either contracted in or in larger corporate organizations done through a department whose function is to maximize the effective use of the owned or leased space.

Of course if you are planning a home office, you will have a lot of preexisting restrictions, some of which we discussed in Chapter 2. Although the simple option is to move the furniture and other items into the room and let the space "evolve," using a room planner makes this process a lot easier and less hard work, especially on the lower back (nothing like moving a heavy desk for the fifth time to make you realize that moving things on paper is a lot less work!).

Several software packages are available that can be used for this, but why buy something you can use for free? Free is just about my favorite price point when I am buying anything (although not so much a favorite when I am selling, but that is a story for a different book).

The retailer Pottery Barn offers an online tool that provides most of the features of the software that you would buy, and unless you are planning some serious reconstruction to build out a space, it is more than adequate for planning out a space effectively (see Figure 6.3). You can find the tool at http://www.potterybarn.com/design-studio/tool/home_offices_room_planner.html.

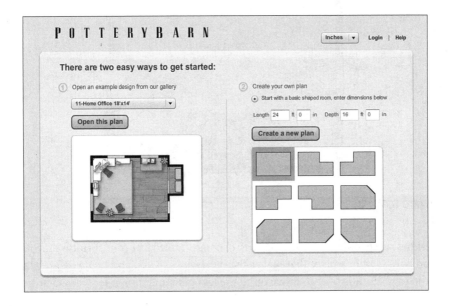

Figure 6.3 *Pottery Barn room planner.*

What I like about this particular tool is that you can start from a basic predesigned plan, or if you are feeling more adventurous, you can start from scratch and enter you own room dimensions, selecting a room shape that roughly matches the one you are planning. Admittedly this is a tool that is designed to sell you Pottery Barn products; therefore, the items that you can place in a room are only those sold by Pottery Barn. However, you can make some very respectable plans by swapping their items for your own as long as you are working with tolerances of several inches rather than exact measurements. Figure 6.4 shows a basic plan of my home office using this tool. As you can see, I was able to place the doors and closet sliding doors accurately, and the major furniture components, even though none of mine were actually bought at Pottery Barn.

Quick disclaimer: This is not an endorsement for Pottery Barn; I simply like their free online tool. I am sure you can find others online or software that you can download or purchase that will fit your own needs. The point here is that planning out a room and the flow of that room is much easier using a tool or even a page of graphing paper than simply moving the furniture around until it fits and hoping that you don't have to move it again!

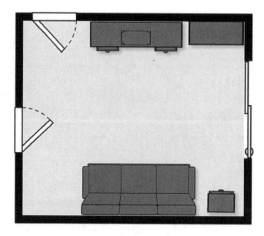

Figure 6.4 *My home office plan.*

Having reached the point where you are comfortable with your furniture layout and have it all in a place that makes the most sense to you and how you are planning to work, it is time to move on to the less permanent or at least easier-to-move items.

One of the most common items for all Out of Office workers is a computer. Of course, the brand, size, and type vary from person to person, and I am most definitely not getting into a discussion of the merits of one brand over another. Some people buy for the task at hand or for the brand; many, I would assume, buy what they can afford.

Where there is a difference is whether or not people use a portable device. Personally, I prefer a desktop computer for my office. I have several reasons for this, but primarily the amount of storage space it offers and the performance. This second factor is diminishing as the performance offered by laptops rapidly catches up and in some cases exceeds that offered by desktops machines. Even with the advances that laptops make, I will probably always use a desktop for my primary machine, and the reason for this is two-fold: the size of screens I can attach to a desktop and the number of screens I can attach. I currently have two screens on my desk: one is 19" the other 26". That makes for a lot of screen space I can utilize. When I do work from a laptop, I struggle with only having a 15" screen on which to view things. Of course, a desktop is totally impractical for traveling with—can you imagine loading one into those little grey trays at the airport? So a laptop has been the only realistic option for many years and for many remains so. However, with the increase in the capabilities offered by tablet devices, this is changing. On shorter trips (anything less than three days), I rarely carry a laptop. I can achieve most of what I need to do on a tablet in that timeframe. On a longer trip, where I will be editing a lot of documents or images, I have to revert to the laptop, but I am confident that in a few years that will no longer be the case and that laptops will become a thing of the past for all but a few power users.

The other thing that takes up a lot of space on my desk is storage. I have a small wooden three-drawer storage box, which one of my monitors sits on, that I picked up in a vintage store. It holds various office supplies, batteries, and other sundries. It's probably not particular practical but it does hold the items I use most regularly, which enables me to be more effective. So, even though there are storage solutions with a smaller footprint, this time form beat out function. After all, if you are going to work in your own space, shouldn't it reflect who you are?

If you take a look at Figure 6.4, my office plan, you can see I have another desk to the right of my main desk. This is actually a small media table that I use to house my printer, paper, and labels. As I mentioned before, having a paper trail that is physical has helped me out on more than one occasion, and so having a printer near at hand makes it much easier to keep that maintained. One feature that I absolutely love about the printer is that it is wireless, which means that I can print from any device that is connected to the wireless network in our home—computer, laptop, iPad, or phone.

That level of convenience actually makes a lot of difference to those working Out of Office from their home. I really find being able to print things directly from my phone an advantage, rather than having to go and look them up on a computer when I remember. Of course, many digital natives will groan at that statement, asking me why I don't use some form of bookmarking system—after all, they are numerous. I'm just that weird mix of digital and analog that likes to read some things on paper whereas other information is just fine being confined to the screen.

Carrying It All with You

So let's assume you have your office space organized. You have the furniture positioned in an optimal way to make you extremely efficient and you know exactly where all your office supplies are—nirvana! Can you carry that level of organization with you when you travel? Let's face it, few of us are in a position where we never travel on business, and for those of us who run our own businesses, even if the travel for business is rare, we usually want to stay connected to the business when we are on vacation (more on that in the next chapter).

So the requirement of being able to take the level of organization that we have achieved in our permanent space with us on the road is something that cannot be ignored. When I travel, for either business or pleasure, for a trip that is longer than one night, I want to be able to set up an office space in my hotel room that at least mimics the basics of my home office. Although I won't be carrying a printer or other major device with me, I do want the ability to remain organized, even in a strange space.

I am amazed at the people I meet on the road who I know to be extremely well organized in their office space yet seem to have no idea where things are when they are on the road. With so much to think of when traveling, having one less thing to think about just makes sense to me. I have spent years trying different bags—in fact, I'm a bit of a collector.

I'm not going to recommend a bag to you. What? Isn't that the point of a book like this, to solve your issues? There is a very good reason why I won't recommend a bag for you; I don't know what you carry. I've had lots of bags recommended to me over the years, and never has one met my needs. Bags are a very personal item in my experience: What works well for one person doesn't necessarily work well for another.

Some people prefer a simple handle; others a cross-body strap and still others (myself included) backpack-style bags. There is no right answer—only the answer that fits your needs most closely. So all that said, I will tell you the solution I have settled on that seems to work best for me.

I carry two bags with me when I am traveling for business: a backpack and a carryon with wheels. The backpack holds my electronics and camera, along with a change of clothes. The latter is a spill-over from the days of checking bags and something I have never felt the need to do away with. The carryon I use has a suit compartment in the lid, which allows me to pack a sport coat or a suit for business. The rest of the bag is taken up with clothes for the trip. Having traveled a lot, I consider myself a fairly light packer and usually can make these two bags stretch for up to eight days. Over that, unless I have access to laundry facilities then I have to resort to a checked bag.

If you want to do away with bags completely, there are several clothing manufacturers who have created clothing items such as sports jackets, overcoats, and so on, that have dozens of pockets that will hold everything from your phone to a tablet device and pretty much everything in between. Although I haven't tested these out personally, I have seen many reports from friends who have and find them to be extremely useful for short trips—although I confess to having my doubts about the durability of these garments and their ability to not end up making you look as though you are wearing a sack with pockets in it. Although style isn't everything, I try not to appear like I just got out of bed when I am traveling.

There are a few items that I have found that make packing and sorting items in my bag easier. One that I highly recommend is the Grid-It by Cocoon. Again this is not a product endorsement; I have simply found this product to be extremely useful. It can be purchased from most online retailers and a few brick-and-mortar ones as well.

The Grid-It is a pad with numerous elastic straps running both horizontally and vertically, forming a grid across it. You can store pretty much any small item in this web. I use it for all the smaller items that go into my bag. I usually have a notebook in it, a pen, an extra memory card for my camera, in fact just about anything that might get lost at the bottom of my bag goes into the Grid-It so that I know exactly where to find it when I am on the road. It is particular useful, if like me, you prefer bags that are basically big open sacks.

Other travelers prefer that their bag be divided into sections that can be organized, and I can completely understand the appeal of that arrangement—I have just never found a bag that was constructed that way that I particularly liked or that was organized in a way that made sense to me.

Whatever you choose, ensuring that you have all the items with you that you are going to need when on the road makes life an awful lot easier. Depending on the length of the trip, the destination (foreign or domestic), and the purpose of the trip, the items you need will vary.

Power chargers are a must, as well as a phone, laptop, and any other device. I also pack a small power strip—a great way to make friends at an airport. Smartphones are replacing many of the smaller devices that someone would have carried only a few years ago. For example, I use the voice recorder on my phone to record some client meetings to ensure that I have captured all the requirements from that meeting; my smartphone has also replaced my compact digital camera, GPS system, and several other small devices that were always with me on a trip. Of course, some things have been added to the things I carry, such as an external battery pack for my phone so that I don't run the risk of depleting the battery while traveling.

Having a small collection of office supplies with you, including smaller versions of the things you use the most in your main office, is also a way I find of reducing travel stress. Staplers, sticky notes, paperclips, in fact all those office supplies come in travel sizes.

If you are traveling on business, you are going to be collecting receipts. Whether you work for a larger organization or yourself, travel expenses have to be recorded. Now, I will be the first to admit I am not the most organized of people when it comes to paperwork, so I won't be claiming to have some amazing system in place for recording business expenses while on the road. Although I am sure there is software or a smartphone app out there for doing just this, I resort to an analog method—an envelope and a paperclip. I simply collect my receipts and clip them together in order, first to last, as the purchases occur. Then they are entered into the accounting software when I get home. Not the most elegant of solutions, but again, I'm more interested in things that work and suit my work style than necessarily selling you on the latest piece of technology. There are plenty of technology evangelists who will happily do that for you.

As with data, I also find redundancy with certain items a must. Also, remembering to rely on the simplest solution is usually the best backup you can find. I am reminded of an old joke about the space program, about how NASA spent a million dollars inventing a pen that would write in space, and the Russian space program simply issued their astronauts with pencils. Just because it is the latest and greatest gadget, app, software, or travel item, don't overlook the obvious and most simple solution. Sure, it might not win you prizes for innovation, but getting the job done will definitely look better than not because you were relying on something that broke down, ran out of power, or simply needed to be upgraded at a critical moment. Those reasons might just be the digital-age version of "the dog ate my homework" excuse from when I was in primary school. What it really says is that you weren't as organized as you needed to be.

For that very reason, as I've mentioned in previous chapters, I still carry a notebook and pencil with me at all times. Yes, I have a smartphone that has apps that can easily replace these two items, and that in turn would make my bag fractionally lighter—which, as anyone who has walked around a massive conference center for eight or more hours will tell you, is definitely a bonus. But I have never had to recharge my notebook or plug in my pencil (yes, I carry a sharpener too).

Whether you started this chapter as a neat-a-holic or as someone a little less organized, I hope having reached the conclusion of the chapter that you have some new ideas about how to improve the efficiency of your workspace and how to carry that efficiency through to your time on the road.

My final piece of advice: Find what works for you. If that is a piece of software, great. If it is an envelope and a pencil, then use that. The point is, be organized anywhere and everywhere, and you will not only reduce your stress levels but you will be much more efficient, and at the end of the day that means you will spend less time working and more time on other things. That, however, is the topic of my next chapter.

Rule Setting

How many times, while reading this book, have you paused to check your phone? Emails, text messages, social media—we are always connected and we expect that we can always gain access to our contacts, business, or social network.

The Connectedness of All Things

This connectedness, which allows us a level of communication that was unimaginable a few years ago, can also become a corral that defines us, limits us, and creates behaviors that would otherwise not exist. We are, at times, almost Pavlovian in our response to the audible and visual notifications that our phones, computers, and other devices send us. We don't want to miss something; we have, in the parlance of the Internet, an "FOMO" (a fear of missing out).

Organizations are morphing along with their employees. A few decades ago, when someone left the office, that was the last contact they had with work until the next business day. Certainly some would take paperwork home, but on the whole the average office worker finished their day, went home, and didn't hear from the office again until the next day.

The arrival of email did little to change that. The emphasis gradually shifted from in-person meetings and telephone calls to the speed and efficiency of email. Then, in 1999 a Canadian company called Research In Motion released a device called The Blackberry—an email pager. That probably marked the turning point for many employees. From this point on, email followed them out of the office. Smartphones appeared in 2003, and email became ubiquitous; no longer tethered to the computer, email was now in the pockets and purses of employees everywhere.

The Blackberry phone became a symbol in many organizations that you had in fact made it. They were issued to members of staff considered important enough to need 24/7 contact with the organization. They became the aspirational symbol of middle managers everywhere. Giving your undivided attention in a meeting was no longer a requirement if you were glancing at your Blackberry; obviously you had important things to focus on.

Ten years later and recent surveys show that American parents feel that 12 is the age at which it is appropriate for children to receive their first mobile phone. This, in terms of high school cool factor, means a smartphone. No longer restricted to the executive, email-enabled phones are in the hands and backpacks of children across the U.S. and in many other countries too.

We have created a 24/7/365 society. Always on, always connected and always ready to respond. The current generation of workers, including those who are just entering the work place, are still too young to have lived solely in this environment. An intern joining a company today would have been 12 or 13 years old when smartphones arrived. Unless they were extremely privileged, they were unlikely to have been among the early adopters of them.

The next generation, however, will have been born into a world where always on is the norm. They will enter the workforce expecting nothing less than to be in constant communication with the organization they work for—not a welcoming prospect for them, if you ask me. Of course, they won't feel this pull in the same way we do, because they will find it natural, just as we find it natural to announce that we are taking "tech breaks" from time to time.

Unplugging—Not the Future

What will "unplugged" mean to that generation? Perhaps it will be a form of punishment, imposed not just by parents but by society itself: the removal of the constant buzzing of communication, the disconnection of a person from their network for a given amount of time. Will the quiet, the isolation be a deterrent? Will they be so addicted to the ability to communicate at all times that the mere thought of not being able to will give rise to paroxysms of fear?

I know a few people, even today, who find the thought of not having their phone in their hand or at least within easy reach quite disturbing; they are unable to maintain conversations without glancing at the screen, and should the device run out of power—or worse still, succumb to some technical malfunction—they are thrown into chaos, usually taking to their favorite social network via a computer to share the horror of not being able to communicate using their phone.

The phone is no longer simply a method of communication, it is a manner of self and group validation. Through the smartphone, the user can share, in real time if they wish, their every waking moment. They can emphasize how great or how badly their life is. They can share the music they are listening to, their location, and images of what they see around them or of the food they are eating. Communication via the phone is no longer restricted to the verbal; it is images, sounds, and the written word.

Shaping Behavior

The workplace has been impacted by this "always on" trend, too. There have always been employees who, when viewed from above, seem to "go the extra mile," or when viewed by peers are seen as indispensable to the organization. Some organizations have taken advantage of this and allowed such employees to take on extra work and avoid taking all their vacation days, thus effectively increasing output without increasing the compensation accordingly.

The Monday-to-Friday 9–5 workweek is a dim memory for most people working at any mid- to large-sized organization (small business owners and entrepreneurs have rarely enjoyed that luxury). The demands on the employee to be as efficient as possible, to "achieve more with less," have increased dramatically over the past decade. Although we are still in a society of hourly waged and salaried staff, the disparity that used to exist between their rates of pay has declined in real terms.

Think through this example: A manual worker, working for a large organization as part of an on-site maintenance team, earns $23 per hour and works, without overtime, 40 hours per week. They receive a gross pay of $920 per week. A salaried worker at the same organization, in junior management, earns $95,000 a year, a gross weekly wage of $1,826—on the surface of it, double the money. However, divide that by 70 and you arrive at an hourly rate of $26 per hour. Where did I get the 70 hours from? I am including all the time spent at home before going to work, the time on the journey home from work, the time in the evenings after work, and the time during the weekends that the average organizational employee spends checking work emails and responding to them outside of "office hours."

Those additional hours are not accounted for. They are not factored into the salary budget, nor are they recompensed directly. Now, of course, there are "perks" designed to offset some of this inconvenience. Perhaps the organization supplies the phone or pays the phone bill and allows any personal use of the phone that the employee wants. Where this happens, though, the organization usually wants to own the device in some manner, either by controlling what apps can be installed or by installing monitoring software on the device to check for usage.

So we have a group of employees who are now perpetually tethered to their organization. Oh, and that maintenance worker, he was issued a smartphone, too—just in case there is an emergency! In effect, what has happened is that organizations have, knowingly or unknowingly (depending on your view of corporations), tapped into the social behavior that was already appearing and commandeered it for their own benefit. In the world of dog training, this is called behavior shaping. This sounds all very sinister and almost conspiracy theory like, doesn't it? Of course, an employee is free to turn off that phone or other device at any time. No one says they have to work the evenings and weekends, but (and here is where it becomes even worse than someone saying it) it is expected, not just by managers but by peers. We are back to the connectedness of our network. Where once we reserved evenings and weekends for family and friends, now work colleagues have the expectation that you can be reached then as well. Peer pressure, as we all have experienced, is a powerful thing. A few Monday morning comments about how someone was hard to reach over the weekend and suddenly you are checking your work email instead of enjoying that walk in the park.

Without wanting to sound like a first-year political science student fresh from their first reading of *Das Kapital* and Marx's theory of the ownership of the means of production, organizations are benefiting from the new social norm of "always on." The toothpaste is out of the tube; what has been unleashed cannot be put away. The change from analog to digital in both the technical sense and the sense of being able to demark and delineate work and personal time has happened and continues to do so. We are probably the last generation of workers who will have a clear memory of what that divide looked and felt like. We might pause for a moment to mourn its passing, but my phone just told me that there was a new email waiting for me so I'll read that instead.

So addicted to our devices are we that social games are being invented to try and hold back the inevitable tide of perpetual connectedness. Phone Stack is one name for the social game where everyone at lunch or dinner puts their mobile phones in a stack on the table. The first person to pick up their phone during the meal has to pick up the tab for the entire meal. As much as a deterrent as paying for an entire table of food might seem, it doesn't deter the most ardent of phone users. In fact, I would hazard to guess that some people would pick up their phone simply to show just how important or how addicted they are—a kind of badge of honor.

Quaint social games will not stem the flood of phone usage, and I am not convinced we should try. Although we are, at the most basic level, becoming slaves to our own machines, it is far more complex than that. We created the systems that have ensnared us, but we have also benefitted greatly from them. The ability to be able to stay in communication with others without being tethered to a location has benefits that, in many cases, outweigh the detriments. The world in which we live and work has and continues to change. Change, it is often said, is the only constant in the human state. Although we might reminisce and even mourn the passing of our "golden age," the lone driver stuck with a broken-down car on the side of a dark highway in the rain is probably very thankful that the small device they carry keeps them connected to the world while help arrives. Sometimes it is only in the absence of something that we truly understand its value. I read recently a story of a group of friends who had decided to take their motorcycles on a vacation trip through Baja Mexico. They had a great time and were on their way back to the United States when they noticed one of their party was missing. The group circled back and found the crashed motorcycle at the side of the road. On first inspection it appeared their friend had died in the accident. No one had a cell phone signal. So they had to sit on the side of the road, with their friend's body for over an hour until a car came along. It was later discovered that the rider had died of dehydration. A poignant story: The phone might not have made a difference, perhaps the rider would not have been revivable had emergency services been called, but what is certain is that the group of riders, with no method of calling for help, were left alone with their thoughts and the body of their friend.

Pros and Cons of Always On

Being always on has its advantages as much as it has disadvantages. I have received, downloaded, and digitally signed contracts while on the road from my mobile device. We can receive news faster and in a more timely fashion than ever before. Standing at the airport watching the information board change the status of your flight to "cancelled" used to be the first you knew of the issue; now your phone, with the right applications installed, can alert you before the status change ever makes it to the board.

More recently, with the ability to stream video with phones, I've seen more people in airport lounges not just making phone calls home but using video conferencing from their phones to stay in touch. My girlfriend and I use it all the time when one of us is on the road. Somehow being able to trade stories of our day and see each other at the same time makes the connection more real than simply hearing a disembodied voice. I'm sure that Alexander Graham Bell would not only approve of the distance his invention has come, in 1891 he actually predicted that it would be possible and sketched out notes on how it might work. From his first phone call, conducted only 100 years after the United States' declaration of independence, to the first video call from the top of Mount Everest a scant 137 years later, the phone has come to dominate our lives, both social and professional.

As I have mentioned in earlier chapters, it is my belief that the mobile phone has been the singularly most impactful piece of technology in modern human history and will continue to shape and change our behavior to such an extent that society as we recognize it today will be unrecognizable in less than 100 years from now. The mobile device (I doubt we will continue to refer to it as a phone for much longer) has already become wearable. Google are experimenting with the Glass project, a system that presents data visually to the wearer of Google Glasses. At present, it still requires a connection to a mobile phone to operate, but wearable technology is the next obvious step in the drive to an always-on society. Beyond that, who knows? But it is not impossible to think that surgical implants will become a reality rather than a science-fiction fantasy.

Some people are utilizing wearable mobile devices to monitor the amount of exercise they take in a day. They then share this data with others in their network or simply store it online with the company who provides the device. Some of these devices are compatible with diet-monitoring apps on phones, adjusting calorie intake based on targets and the amount of exercise. No longer do we need to consult with a dietician to get what was once specialized information. Now our devices can tell us when we have eaten enough, when we need more exercise, and how we are doing compared to our network. We have turned what was once a private struggle to maintain, lose, or gain weight into a competitive activity, a game to be played with those we know and sometimes with those we don't.

With all this access, constant connectedness, and overwhelming pressure to share everything about our lives, how do we set rules in place that mean we are actually leading a life and not constantly in work mode?

I am not referring here to the creation of a work/life balance: I tackle that topic in the next chapter. What I am referring to is the set of rules you need to create to maintain your individuality and your corporate identity and to establish healthy relationships, both professional and personal. The blurring of these lines is, in my opinion, one of the root causes of so much daily stress: the feeling that one must sacrifice one thing in order to achieve another. How many times have you said or heard said that there just aren't enough hours in the day?

Economists refer to this as "opportunity cost," which is the price paid for making a choice between two or more options. That is all well and good in the dry and somewhat esoteric world of finance lecture, but here we are talking about people and their lives. How do we achieve a life in which the price we pay is acceptable to all parties?

There is no truly easy formula for this, and I'm certainly not going to try and convince you otherwise. There are, however, steps that can be taken that I believe will move you closer to achieving this goal. What follows is one of those steps.

Creating a Rule Book

In this section, I outline five rules that I believe to be the core of the set of rules you will create for yourself. These rules are a distillation of what I have found to be true from my own experiences and the experiences of others who have worked Out of Office for some time. These may seem less like rules for successful working and more like truisms, and in a way they are, but however you choose to view them, they have been an essential ingredient to the successful way not only I but many others have led this type of life for a lot of years.

These five rules are not some mysterious knowledge being released to you for the first time. Much of it is, as with so much other guidance, common sense. However, although much it is common sense, it seems to escape the common person at the time they most need it, hence the inclusion of these rules in this book.

I have found that having different rule sets for different situations helps me; others find that having one long set of rules works better for them. Whichever camp you fall into, I strongly suggest that you return to this chapter after you have finished the book (or immediately re-read the chapter, if that works for you) and think through your list(s). Don't believe that you will get around to it at some point. Rule setting is a strong advantage for those working Out of Office, and the sooner you create your rule set, the sooner you will start enjoying this work style even more.

Start with the basics and fill in the blanks as they become apparent. Your rule set should be both a reference and a guide, but it should not be inflexible. Your rules will change over time; they will change to meet new conditions and experiences, just as they do in all aspects of your life. However, creating the rules for how you will be successful in working Out of Office is the first step in actually being successful in this style of work.

Rule One

Understand that you are not as indispensable as you believe. Contrary to what you would like to think about yourself, the organization you work for, whether a large corporation or your own business, will continue without you. If you run your own business, as an entrepreneur one of your responsibilities is to ensure that you are able to take breaks from the business without it suffering. That requires timing and a good relationship with your clients—hopefully something you already have established.

If you work for a larger organization, then the belief you are indispensable often comes from a fear of wondering if you will miss out on something major happening in your absence. This feeling can be compounded for those who work Out of Office. Because of the separation between the Out of Office worker and their in-office counterparts the added distance of being incommunicado can lead to an enhanced feeling of isolation. Rather than relaxing during downtime, stress can increase as the mind runs wild with imaginings of organizational changes, promotions, downsizing, lucrative client accounts being swapped, and blame being laid at the door of the absentee.

If you are suffering from these types of worries when you are disconnected from your organization, then I humbly suggest that you might be working for the wrong organization. This type of fear, experienced by many more than would care to admit it, can be soul destroying. I have known several sales-based organizations that deliberately create this type of working environment to keep people "keen." Of course, that is really a smoke screen for what they are actually doing, which is using up the resource available at the time and replacing it as required with "new blood."

Now I am not suggesting that everyone who has these feelings is in fact working for the evil empire. For some of us, these fears are borne out of nothing more than half-perceived slights, a lack of sleep, and a desire to truly do the very best job we can—the thought of not being perceived that way can be worrying and cause a downward spiral of similar thoughts.

The rule here is to accept that there is a difference between being a valued employee or vendor and being indispensable—that taking time away from thinking only about your job actually broadens you as a human being and enables you to contribute more to your work life, which in turn makes you more valuable. So rather than you diminishing your value to your organization or clients, taking time away, if used effectively, will actually increase your value.

Rule Two

There is a difference between being flexible and being a doormat. No one appreciates intransigence; a lack of ability or willingness to adapt to changing requirements or situations is a friction point in any organization, regardless of size. When I was in the military, there was a clause attached to almost every concession granted: "unless counter to the exigencies of the service." This meant that while you might be granted a weekend pass or a posting that you had applied for, if that situation changed and they needed you elsewhere, then elsewhere was where you would be. The military is an extreme example of an ecosystem that does not suit everyone, nor is it suited to running a business. However, the caveat included in those concessions transfers well to many business settings. The issues only arise when those with the authority to change requirements do so without thought or empathy for those affected. This can range from changing the requirements of a project to overloading an employee with work.

The Out of Office worker can become the victim of this type of mismanagement simply because they are perceived as being more flexible. They work from home and manage their own time at a level of granularity that is different from their co-workers, so they should be able to cope better with changes and increased demands—so the thinking goes.

Although it may well be true that Out of Office workers are more flexible, it does not follow that they are any more capable of dropping everything and changing course than their in-office counterparts. A routine that has been established, even if it is out of a home-based office, is still a routine, and human beings like routines. One of the themes that came through when talking to people who work Out of Office was the enjoyment of being "left alone," not in a literal sense necessarily but in the sense that they were not micromanaged. They enjoyed being the masters of their own work day and deciding the work that should be prioritized.

When this ability is taken away from them because of a sudden (and unnecessary) change, which is disguised as a business requirement, it often leads to stress and resentment. After all, this person has proven themselves capable of working remotely and managing their own time and workflow, so why should they respond well to sudden impositions?

Again, I am using an extreme example here to illustrate the point. Not every change of direction or need for someone to work the weekend is simply a power play by some bored executive. In many cases, there is a genuine business need. Take, for example, the situation with Yahoo! and their CEO Marisa Mayer. I have been asked by some people who knew I was writing a book on this topic for my thoughts on her decision to remove Out of Office working from that organization. First of all, I don't know the full situation at Yahoo!, and, second, I've never worked there, so I'm not qualified to make a full assessment. But my feeling was that this was a decision that was made in the best interests of the business and not a knee-jerk reaction because someone didn't like the thought of people working away from the office. It was a genuine business need as the company underwent restructuring.

So the rule here is to learn to recognize when there are genuine reasons for business needs that require adaptability and learn when to push back and have your own space and time respected. Just because you work Out of Office doesn't mean you are on call 24/7 (unless that is your job). Sometimes you are going to have to be on a conference call at 3 a.m., and sometimes you might be on a video call at 11 p.m. Those are the requirements of many jobs that have a global slant to them.

But you know that going into it. The message here is that Out of Office working doesn't make you the go-to person for all of those types of situations simply because there is a perception that you work in your pajamas anyway.

Rule Three

It's called work, not lying on the beach, for a reason. It can be tempting to become too relaxed working in your own space. Showers at 4 p.m., working on a laptop in front of the TV, spending the day running errands using your smartphone to give the appearance of being in the office—all these things happen to Out of Office workers. These might sound like stereotypes and fuel for reasons why management is loath to allow staff to work in this way, but stereotypes come from somewhere and have their root in truth or at least a sliver of it.

Just as it is important for you to set rules to ensure you are not taken advantage of, so too it is important for you to set rules of your own that ensure you don't take advantage of the situation you find yourself in. As mentioned in previous chapters, self-discipline is one of the biggest requirements for working successfully Out of Office. There are a greater number of temptations in this work style than in any other. It is important to recognize that there is a difference between managing your time and taking advantage of the time you have. I am not a great believer in trading time or tasks for other opportunities; it is just too easy to become indebted to your own schedule—or worse, your organization's schedule. Of course, it is tempting to go and see a popular movie at an afternoon matinee; after all, you can always work a few hours later in the evening to ensure the work is done. I have a movie theatre across the street from me, literally no more than five minutes from my door. They even serve food at your seat, and the seats are wide and very comfortable. I am also an avid movie-goer. It would be all too easy for me to trade off some tasks and go to the movies in the afternoon. I choose not to do that, not because I am a paragon of virtue but because I set myself rules. Some things are viable trade-offs; for example, getting the grocery shopping done so my girlfriend doesn't have to do it on her way home from work—that is a valuable trade-off because it means we get more time together in the evenings. I can also do it during my "lunch break."

In other words, the rule is about not abusing your Out of Office work style. Why is this important? I actually believe it has implications beyond just your own routine, or the impact you might have on the organization you work for. I ride a motorcycle. I often see other motorcyclists weaving in and out of traffic, cutting in front of car drivers and generally abusing the rules of the road. It might be excused as them having some fun. The problem is that the car driver who just had a bike roar past him making them brake suddenly is now going to view all motorcyclists the same way—as a nuisance. That means the next time they ought to yield to a bike, they may choose not to, and that next time it might be me on the bike. The same is true for Out of Office workers who "bend" the rules to suit themselves. They can ruin the opportunity for others who are in the same position. Back to the Yahoo! story: One of the reasons cited in the thinking behind bringing all staff into the office by Marisa Mayer was that some members of staff had set up their own businesses while working Out of Office for Yahoo!. That is definitely more than bending the rules; that is pretty much throwing them out of the window. This is just one example of a few people ruining the experience for many others. Would you want to be the person at your organization that was part of the reason that a sweeping change like this took place? I know I certainly wouldn't.

The rules and playing by them help establish the trust that is needed by both sides for the Out of Office work style to be successful. Without trust, it is hard to have a successful relationship, personal or professional. Rules help everyone understand the boundaries and establish how trust is earned.

I am not saying that you have to be tied to your desk 9–5 Monday to Friday. Out of Office working comes with flexibility and a reduction in rigidity, but there have to be rules. I personally think it is better to impose rules on yourself than have others impose them on you.

At the end of the day, if you can honestly say you accomplished all that you needed to do, then it was probably a good day and your work rule is operating as it should be, even if you did manage to sneak in a matinee showing of the latest blockbuster!

Rule Four

Communicate the rules. Okay, so you have created a set of rules that work for you and your organization or clients. Don't keep them to yourself. Share them, especially with those around you who might be tempted to break them if they don't know about them or understand them. For the Out of Office worker, that includes anyone you share your domestic space with.

In Chapter 4, "Working from Home," I covered the different challenges that working from home can create. As I mentioned there, it is important to have clear boundaries that everyone in the space understands. If you have your own office in a room in the house, treat it like an office—don't let it also become a junk store or a second play room for the kids. Equally, if your office doubles up as a guest room, think ahead when you know you have guests coming to stay: What will you need to move out of the office so that you can remain productive?

My office is also our guest room; we don't have a lot of people stay over, but once a year my daughters visit from the UK for at least a week, sometimes longer. That means I have to prepare in advance to make sure that the room is comfortable for them and that I can still be productive during their visit.

Although not ideal, it can be done, but only if you plan ahead and have some rules in place about how the room is treated when it is in use as your office.

The same is true of your time. As I mentioned in Rule Three, setting rules about how you spend your time is important in ensuring that you maintain productivity and effectiveness as an Out of Office worker. But there is more to it than that. Setting rules that your domestic partners understand and that you have effectively communicated reduces friction and ensures that your time is respected—which is why it is important for you to respect your time as well. It really isn't going to be great if you have a rule in place that says you can't do grocery shopping on Wednesdays because of your schedule but you decide you can make that matinee showing. There is a conflict in your rules. Make sure your rules make sense to everyone.

Equally, communicate your rule set to those you work with, whether they are co-workers or clients. If you have children and it is your responsibility to pick them up from school at 4 p.m. every day, then make sure that you have communicated to your co-workers and clients that they should not expect you to be on a conference call at that time. If people understand the reason in advance, they are usually a lot more willing to work with the rule than if they are not informed, at least in my experience.

Rule Five

Rules are for breaking. Yes, I know that sounds contradictory—after all, didn't I just spend several pages—and more than a few minutes of your life while you read those pages—outlining why you should have rules and what you might include in that rule set?

The point here is that you cannot foresee every circumstance. As much as you might plan out your day, week, month, or quarter, there will always be circumstances that you haven't planned for—surprises, some good, some not so good, that put a twist into your schedule. One of my clients recently had a conference organized for some of their customers. It had taken weeks to plan, everything was in place, vendors were recruited to put on an expo, and speakers were booked; everything, down to the coffee breaks, was mapped out.

Then, just two days before the event, the city in which the conference was to take place was bombed. The city was Boston and the conference had been scheduled to take place at MIT. How do you put in place a rule for that? Simple answer, you don't.

That is where breaking the rules has an advantage. There are times when going to see that matinee showing can be the best thing you can do for yourself at that time.

I'm going to look at self-care in more detail in the next chapter, but self-care is and should be a priority for you. You are not a machine; you are a frail living organism, and you need constant maintenance. The ability to adapt and cope with change is balanced by our need to feel in control.

Sometimes life conspires or at least seems to conspire against us to remove that control. How do you think the event organizer felt when canceling the Boston event? Weeks of preparation had gone into the event but at the same time lives had been lost, families devastated, others seriously injured. On the grand scale of things, did the event really matter? Measured on that scale, of course, it didn't, but on a smaller scale, on a scale of personal time spent, yes it did. However, no one can share that scale with you. It is your scale against which you measure things. In that situation, how can you possibly share your disappointment at not being able to see something you had planned not come to fruition. If you give voice to your disappointment, then you are likely to be perceived as petty by co-workers and clients alike. But even the most resilient of us would draw a sigh as we canceled something we had spent time and effort on.

So, you need to break the rules from time to time. Maintain your sanity, keep your effectiveness, and break the rules—just do it with a clear conscience.

When you draw up your list of rules—and, yes, I highly recommend making them a physical list—try not to be too loose or too restrictive. Most certainly don't be too unrealistic. If you know that you are not a morning person, then making a rule that the work day starts at 7 a.m. every day is going to be a rule that is constantly broken—and although I support you breaking rules every now and then, why make a rule that you will be unable to honor?

While being realistic, think about the other restrictions on your time and the obligations you have to others, be they partners, clients, or co-workers. Think about rules that make your relationships with them easier to manage. If they are included in your rule set, they are much more likely to both support the rules that help you most and be more aware of them.

I have rules that I communicate to event organizers when I am being booked as a speaker: They are in my contract. These rules make my life a little easier when I am on the road: They include which airlines I will and will not fly, which hotels I prefer to stay in (not, as you might imagine, the most expensive ones), what time of day and evening I am prepared to fly, and so on. This might look like a diva list to some, but by having a set of rules and clearly communicating them before reaching an agreement, I ensure everyone knows what to expect.

The same is true for Out of Office workers who are employed by organizations and interact with co-workers. Setting rules about when you can and cannot be reasonably expected to be contacted helps a lot with managing expectations. Remember, though, that rules that involve other people are best written as part of a negotiation, not simply handed out as though they were a set of commandments.

As you have probably noticed, a lot of my rules revolve around communication. In my experience, the largest number of issues arise, both in social and professional interactions, when communication breaks down. A lack of understanding, a misreading of intent, or a phrase that is used in an unfamiliar way, can wreak havoc on the best of relationships.

My recommendation is to start with a rule set that covers communication, for both your personal and work relationships, and defines communication styles, methods, and timings. Then work outward from there, creating new rule sets for the individual circumstances you find yourself in.

It may sound somewhat regimented and restrictive to some, but I can assure you that once you have created these rules, you will not regret having done so. You will find that you are more efficient, you can manage expectations better, and those around you have a better understanding of when you are going to be available to them.

The point of setting rules is not to fence you in but to free you. So when you review your rules, try to view them from that perspective. Keep your rules handy; put them somewhere you will see them on a regular basis.

That isn't to say that they should be so complex that they need to be studied like a law book; however, having reminders is another way to shape your own behavior and that of others. Gently remind people of your rules. I've seen people do this in all kinds of ways, including one of my favorites: via the signature block of their email. This can be a simple note mentioning your availability that week or a reminder to clients that invoices are due on a particular date.

The rules don't have to be trumpeted from the rooftops, and I will reiterate again: Don't be rigid about them. Gentle reminders go a long way to sustaining the practice of rule setting. If either side abandons the rules, there was no real point in creating them in the first place.

So grab a notebook and pen and start your list of rules. The sooner you start, the easier it will be. Ask your co-workers, clients, and partners to help you construct a realistic and achievable set of rules. Encourage them to write their own set of rules so that you can respect their time and work more fully.

8

Work/Life Integration

Webster's dictionary defines balance as "a beam that is supported freely in the center and has two pans of equal weight suspended from its ends." It's succinct and to the point. Now apply that to the phrase "work/life balance." It implies that the two things, work and life, can be made to become of equal weight, and having achieved that you can get to a point where they balance.

I've been working ever since I left school more than 30 years ago. I have had jobs that I hated, jobs that left me exhausted, and jobs that I couldn't wait to get to every day. The one thing I have never had is a job that carried equal weight to the rest of my life. My children, my partner—those are the things that are important to me. Those things will always outweigh work in my life.

I understand that for some people their careers are incredibly important, and finding a way to ensure that they spend equal amounts of time and energy on both their personal lives and their professional lives is a goal that they strive for on a daily basis. I've seen a lot of professionals take on this challenge, but I've yet to see any of them successfully manage it. There might be brief moments where they achieve some measure of equilibrium, but for the most part that is an illusion, mostly borne from the fact that they are too exhausted from trying to get everything in balance.

Balancing Act

I truly believe that attempting to balance your professional life and your personal life is at best a fool's errand and at worst detrimental to both. The fact that we refer to the balance as work/life should tell us something. Work is work, but everything outside work is, in fact, life. I understand that not everyone gets to do what they love. I consider myself extremely fortunate to be in a position that I not only work but also I love what I do and therefore it doesn't actually seem like work. For example, this section of this particular chapter is being written on the couch on a quiet Sunday morning while the rest of the house is asleep. Not everyone gets that luxury.

However, the demarcation between work and life is perhaps at the root of the balancing act that so many attempt and yet fail at. Can you ever truly achieve a balance between two things that are unequal in your own perception?

As I discussed in the last chapter, the level of technology we have achieved in today's world means that we are always connected. It means that many of us have to make a conscious effort to be disconnected, whereas only a few years ago the reverse was true. We would have to make an effort to remember to check email; now we have to make a conscious effort to remember to check for physical mail.

Achieving a balance between two different areas of your life entails the ability to clearly classify activities that fall into those two areas. For example, when you pick up your cell phone that has both work and personal email accounts on it, can you only check one or the other? During working hours, are you going to ignore personal messages? During "nonworking" hours, are you only going to read personal messages?

If you bring your laptop home from the office, are you seriously going to be able to let it sit in the bag it was carried home in, or are you going to power it up to finish off that project? Defining what constitutes work hours and what constitutes life hours is a complex issue for many individuals. The pull of unfinished work, that gnawing at the back of your mind that reminds you that it will be waiting for you in the morning competes for attention with your child's homework, your partner's retelling of their day, a favorite television show, a family meal, your dog that needs walking, and a million other "life" tasks.

Priorities

Another way that many look at this so-called "balancing act" is to prioritize elements of both lives. I think of this as just another version of the attempt to balance things until they have equal value. Let's think through what prioritizing life elements actually means.

To prioritize items you first have to rank them in some kind of order. Usually this takes the form of an order of importance. When you divide the two realms, work and life, the prioritization becomes a little easier. Your child's homework assignment can be ranked above walking the dog, helping your partner prepare the evening meal can be ranked above watching TV, and so on. Likewise with work tasks, you know which tasks need to take precedence for your job to be completed effectively. Now how do you match those two lists to achieve balance?

Does completing that work task take precedence, carry more weight, or come higher on the list of priorities than helping your child with their homework? Is it more important to help prepare dinner than to check work email for that one item you need to finish the day's work tasks?

These are all, of course, personal decisions. I'm certainly not going to try and tell you what your priorities should be. The point is to illustrate just how hard making those types of decisions can be. I certainly can't imagine trying to prioritize between work tasks and spending time with a child.

Some people find these decisions to be "sacrifice" based. You sacrifice time with your child now so that you can ensure their future. I can see the justification in that, although the concept seems a little like borrowing from one account to pay a bill owed from another. Of course, different cultures view time with family, time spent at work, and the decisions that have to be made about which to prioritize differently. In some cultures, the notion of sacrificing time with family is completely alien; in others it is not even considered a sacrifice.

Whether you view it as a sacrifice, an opportunity cost, or as a natural order of things, there can be no doubt that we, as an ordinary human beings, cannot be in two places at once and that most of us find it extremely difficult to focus our attention on more than one task at a time. Can you be really present with your partner and respond to emails? Can you help your child with homework and at the same time be on a conference call?

The Myth of Multitasking

It is a commonly accepted claim in today's society that as our dependency on technology has risen, our ability to multitask has risen along with it. This is, of course, a myth. Multiple research studies conducted over the past few decades continue to show that the ability of human beings to multitask is extremely limited and that the quality of any output or concentrated thought declines as more tasks are added.

Jordan Grafman, chief of the Cognitive Neuroscience Section at the National Institute of Neurological Disorders and Stroke (NINDS), is quoted as saying:

> You're doing more than one thing, but you're ordering them and deciding which one to do at any one time.

In other words, our attempt at multitasking is really a prioritization of actions. The myth of multitasking has increased with the popular culture acceptance of the "geek," at least in Western societies. A term that was originally derogatory is now "cool," and along with it the associated faux-technical knowledge and language of the geek. Multitasking originated as a computer term, referring to the way in which early computers appeared to be able to manage more than one calculation at a time. This was also only an appearance provided because of the speed at which the calculations were performed. Human beings are not capable of this level of speed.

Perhaps the most common example of multitasking, and one that has led to an increasing number of jurisdictions banning the practice, is that of texting and driving. The argument that being able to text and drive was the same multitasking process as driving while holding a conversation or driving and listening to the radio was discounted, and it is now illegal to text and drive or, in fact, use any of the non-voice-based applications on a smartphone while driving.

So if we, as a society, accept that we are not able to safely operate a vehicle and use a phone at the same time, why do we insist that we are able to divide our attention in ways that, although less hazardous, can still damage us, if only at the relationship level? Our hubris regarding the ability we think we have to multitask has, in my opinion, led to the type of thinking that leads us to believe we are capable of balancing work and life.

Let me provide another example. Often someone who has a lot of tasks to complete at the same time is said to have "a lot of plates spinning at once." The phrase relates to the circus or street performer act of placing plates on the top of flexible poles and using the flexibility of the poles to keep the plates spinning at the top so that they don't fall to the ground and break.

However, the performer only has one pair of eyes and one pair of hands. So their success is determined by their ability to see which plates are slowing down and increase the spin of those that need it, while quickly moving to the next set of plates. At best, the performer can spin two plates at the same time. The overall effect maybe that they have a dozen plates spinning at once but in fact they are rapidly moving from one set of plates to the next. Instead of multitasking, they are prioritizing based on need; they are judging which plate is about fall.

Many of us apply this process to our work lives and indeed our personal lives. The failure comes when we try and manage both lives using the same process. It is simply not possible to manage two different lives in this way, at least in my experience.

So if a work/life balance is impossible to achieve, what is the solution?

Integration, Not Balance

I prefer the concept of *work/life integration*, which moves away from the idea of separateness and espouses a whole life approach. The first part of this whole life approach is to give up the concept of balance, of trying to provide equal weight to tasks from two different lives. Instead, each task, activity, or job plays an equal part in the whole of a person's life.

That can be a hard concept for some people to adjust to. How can work be as important as home? Or email as important as a child's homework? In a literal sense, as I've already mentioned in this chapter, I don't think they are. However, in terms of integrating what was previously considered two separate lives into one whole, they become equal.

Instead of trying to apportion a weight or value to a task (for example, walking the dog is a lower priority than answering work email), integration means that we apportion time throughout our day to attend to various tasks that need doing. The first loss after successfully transitioning to a whole life integration is guilt.

How many times have you felt guilty because you couldn't play with your child because you were working on a project at home? How many times have you had to skip a social arrangement with friends because you had to deal with emails? If you have been working any length of time, I would venture to say that you have experienced a situation like this at least once, and of course felt the associated guilt that goes with making that prioritization.

By not making those tradeoffs, by not trying to prioritize one task over another in terms of importance, you are less likely to feel guilty about which task you choose to do. Less guilt, less stress; less stress, improved efficiency. Almost sounds too good to be true—and you know what they say about things that sound too good to be true, right?

I am not suggesting that this is some secret, never-before-revealed method of achieving a stress-free life. If you have that secret, please share it with me! What I am suggesting is that by abandoning the idea of prioritizing tasks based on their perceived importance and moving to a new paradigm of integrating tasks into the day, you can simplify your life and reduce the guilt and stress of managing your day.

In reality, this is really only possible for the Out of Office worker. Those workers who are in-office only are stuck with the value-based prioritization method that so many of us are familiar with. This is just another benefit of the Out of Office work style.

No More Priorities

So if you aren't going to prioritize tasks based on a value system, then what are the alternatives? The Out of Office work style provides options—at its core, that is why both individuals and organizations choose to utilize it. Perhaps the biggest of the options it provides, and one that is both obvious and yet greatly overlooked by many, is the flexibility of time.

How you utilize time changes completely when you are working Out of Office. There are, of course, a few constraints, but for the most part they are conventions rather than necessities. I first started to realize this when working for a company that had its headquarters in India. Because of the time difference of 10.5 hours between us, it was necessary for the whole team to be flexible. For the most part, my colleagues in India worked a U.S.-based shift. However, that wasn't always possible, nor was it practical, and at times I would need to be available to them during their daytime, which corresponds to evening or early morning in the U.S.

Adjusting my working day to meet the needs of my team meant that I was either up a lot earlier than my U.S.-based colleagues and clients or working a lot later. However, this time-shifting meant that I was able to complete tasks and still have my day ahead of me, even if it meant I was ready for bed earlier than usual.

By managing my own day, deciding what time to allocate to which tasks, I was freed from the chore of having to prioritize tasks based on value. Rather, I was able to decide that if, by 2 p.m. I needed to take a nap, then that was going to be okay because it fit into the timeline that I had allocated for myself. When you are solely based in-office, your day is mapped out for you. There is an expectation that you will be in the office at sometime between 7.30 a.m. and 9.30 a.m. and that you will leave at sometime between 5.00 p.m. and 7.00 p.m.

No More Weekends

These parameters are the binding points for your timeline. They are the points between which you must allocate all of your tasks and, with the exception of rare days, provide no time for anything other than work. Is it any wonder that people celebrate Wednesday as "hump day" or announce on social media sites "TGIF"? When faced with days that are out of your control, at least from the perspective of allocating time, the feeling that you do not have real control over your life can be oppressive.

That makes it sound like everyone who works in an office considers it to be somewhat akin to a prison sentence, which of course is not the case, and I don't mean to imply that because someone works in an office with a set timetable that they are drones and not free to set their own priorities. In fact, the opposite is true, but it is still setting priorities based on a value system—usually the value of a time-based deadline or based on the position in the organization of the person who set the task.

How often in your career have you encountered a situation where either yourself or colleagues have been confused by "changing priorities" because somewhere further up the chain of command someone decided that a new task had more value to the organization than a previously assigned one? There are times when it seems that there is a competition being engaged in by managers to see who can assign new values to tasks first, on a daily basis.

The product of this value-based decision making and priority setting is that people are faced with increasingly shortened deadlines, even unrealistic deadlines, and are being asked to produce work at a rate that is not sustainable, perhaps even giving the impression that they have been set up for failure. Although money is the life-blood of any organization, whether for-profit or non-profit, time is the currency of people.

This is often where the conflict within organizations and within people themselves occurs. Work is, at its most basic level, the exchange of time for money. When you hire me to work for your organization, you are offering to exchange your money for my time. Of course, there are certain caveats included as part of that contract of exchange. For example, during the time that I trade for your money I will produce something that has value to you. This concept is true whether you work for an organization or yourself through clients.

It is my opinion that this is why we cannot successfully balance work and life. One is based on money and the other on time. At various points in our life, one or the other has greater value to us, but at no point do they ever have the same value.

When we are younger and just starting out on our careers, money holds a greater value than time. We are looking to establish ourselves in the world, perhaps to buy our first car or our first home, pay off student loans, or meet other financial obligations. As we grow older, perhaps have a family or develop other interests beyond just work, we increasingly value our time more. We want time to enjoy the fruit of our labors, as the old saying goes. So the equation has changed, where we once valued money more than time, we now value time more than money.

So we find ourselves in a position of unbalanced priorities. A business, on the other hand, being only a conceptual existence, only values that which provides continuity—money. Whether you are the CEO of a Fortune 500 company or the owner of a single-person small business, without money, without a steady cash-flow, your business will cease to exist.

So if the organization values money and you switch your values between money and time, how can you balance or prioritize them? At the most basic of levels, the response is simply that without the job you won't earn money, without money you won't be able to afford to enjoy your time away from work, so work must be the priority.

It seems that many people come to the same conclusion; in fact, it seems almost an ingrained, accepted truth. In the U.S., people are persuaded that attending college is the most important step in securing their future. However, in doing so they often enter a ridiculous cycle. To attend college takes money, so they have two choices: Take longer to get their degree as they work to pay for the cost of college, or at least reduce the amount of money they will need to borrow to pay for it, or take on a large debt to pay for their education, a debt that will take them several decades to pay off.

So the joke becomes that a person should attend college so that they can secure a job that will allow them to pay off the debt they incurred by attending college! This seems a very circular arrangement and one that only appears to benefit the educational organizations and those providing the loans. I am not devaluing education by any means here, but again we are in a situation where we have placed value on time that is money based. A student agrees to exchange their time, time spent in learning, in return for paying an educational establishment with money they have borrowed. They are then in a position where they must exchange their time having left education to earn money so they can repay that loan. What would happen, what does happen, when they choose not to make that exchange?

A Fair Exchange

For some, not making this exchange means that they have to select work that has a more manual focus or perhaps a more vocational nature. But that is not always the case. There are many examples of people who have decided not to make that exchange but who went on to build amazing organizations of their own. Richard Branson, the British entrepreneur, only completed high school and had difficulty with that. Bill Gates (co-founder of Microsoft), Michael Dell (founder of Dell Computers), Steve Jobs (co-founder of Apple), and many others never obtained a college degree. They decided to exchange their time for a different set of priorities, and one of the products was, of course, to generate vast fortunes. However, they also built large organizations employing thousands of individuals. If they had not decided to view the method of exchange differently, they would have had very different stories to tell. So it is not impossible to view the system of priorities based on value exchange differently, but it's just not the norm. However, working Out of Office was not the norm a few decades ago, and so if you are going to do something that is not the norm, shouldn't you embrace that type of thinking completely?

Working Out of Office should be more than a change of location. Simply replacing the formal setting of an office with a home-based office, coffee shop, hotel room, or airport lounge isn't fully embracing the entire concept, nor is it exploiting the full advantage that comes with this type of work style. To fully embrace the Out of Office work style requires a changing in thinking. It requires that you change how you approach the day and indeed the other units of time that we are so fond of using as reference points.

I no longer think in terms of a "work" week. There is no Monday to Friday with a weekend to demark the beginning and end of work. This is true of many Out of Office workers. Telecommuters who travel on Sunday evenings to be at a client site for Monday morning, for example, might take back those hours spent at an airport by not being available on a Friday afternoon.

But it goes far beyond that when you really start to embrace the new way of looking at time. If the concept of work tasks being bound by Monday to Friday is no longer relevant, that also means that family and pleasure time are no longer bound by the concept of the weekend. There is no more pressure to try and fit in family and friends and leisure into a 48-hour period, while at the same time dreading the arrival of Monday morning and wishing for just a few more hours of enjoyment.

One of my favorite authors, Douglas Adams, wrote in his humorous science-fiction book *The Hitchhiker's Guide to the Galaxy*, "Time is an illusion, lunchtime doubly so." I won't try and explain the reason that one of his characters says this in the book, but the concept of time being an illusion is, for me, a truism.

I used to be tied to a wristwatch. I was lost without it. I still collect them and wear them for special occasions, but now they are more accessories than essentials. I will even wear a favorite watch if it has stopped if it goes with an outfit I am wearing. Its ability to tell me the time is no longer relevant to my decision to wear it or not. The mobile phone has replaced my watch; it tells me the time and reminds me of appointments if I need reminding. But on an average day, working from home, I will barely look at it for the time. We have several clocks in the house, and I'm sure you have some of the same ones—DVRs, kitchen appliances, and other devices that also provide a clock. I hardly register them. My day is not dominated by a time-piece, but rather by the flow of the day. That is not to say I am without the need to keep track of the day, but rather keeping track of it is more for the benefit of certain routines, such as feeding my cats—although they would hardly let me miss their meals quietly! Of course, there are client calls and meetings that have to be scheduled, and for those keeping track of time is important.

Stop Watching the Clock

On the whole, though, I mostly operate without the constraints of a clock. I get up in the morning; I tackle the tasks that seem most necessary at that time. In some ways, it is a way of living Maslow's hierarchy of needs. Deal with the basics first (food, shelter, warmth, and so on) and then move to the next level of needs. Some days I will work until well into the night. Other days I might stop work at midday and not do any further work until the next day.

This is not some idyll that I have managed to create for myself, but rather a different system of life integration. Working is now as much a part of my daily life as eating, washing, cleaning, reading, entertainment, or any number of other ways I might allocate time. The time to do things is determined less by an opportunity cost model—the concept that if I do one thing, I am sacrificing the opportunity to do something else—and more by when I have completed one thing I will simply move to the next thing. The things might be work items or they might be leisure items. They might be consecutive or mingled.

When I first started working this way, it was hard to remain focused; at first it felt like I was using a reward-based system to determine my day. If I work on this, then I can do this pleasure thing. That strikes me as being a flawed system in much the same way as some diets allow cheat days. If you are cheating on a diet, then the food becomes a reward. If you are rewarding yourself with leisure time, you have resorted to measuring work and leisure as different types of time.

That can be borne out of a lack of enjoyment from your work, of course. For that there is only one cure—find something you love to do, then, as the saying goes, you will never work a day in your life. Perhaps that is the key to being the most successful Out of Office worker: You must love what you do. Certainly it is key to being able to fully integrate all types of time into one experience. If you begrudge the time you spend on a certain task and it becomes a chore, you will certainly view it as an opportunity cost.

There are tasks that I do with no relish; I would be lying if I tried to convince you otherwise. Scooping a full cat litter box at 6 a.m. while still trying to shake the sleep from my eyes is not exactly my idea of a fun time. However, it is not measured against the time I could have spent doing something else. It simply needs doing. It is one task in a day of tasks. Working Out of Office allows me to order those tasks into a day. Equally, there are work-based tasks I get no enjoyment from (invoicing, for example). Yes, it means I get paid, but the whole process of keeping accounts is not something I enjoy doing. I am certain that there are tasks in your job you would prefer not to do. However, if you view them as simply one task among many, the amount you dislike them declines or at least is balanced against the ones you do like.

Integration is about finding the right place in your routine for individual tasks. Some tasks that you undertake, especially those that are work focused, will have impacts on work colleagues. This means that they have to be undertaken and completed by a certain time. This is where the discipline I discussed early in the book comes into play—the discipline to complete tasks when they are due but also to not drift into the old way of thinking, of seeing one set of tasks as being work and the other set of tasks being pleasure.

There is a difference between a task having a due point in time and a task being exchanged for time. Many tasks are time sensitive or at least have a need-based element to them. Children, pets, even ourselves need to be fed at regular intervals. Laundry needs to be done. Your home needs to be cleaned. Groceries need to be bought. These tasks are all need based and to some extent or another time sensitive. Some you may enjoy, others you may not, but you do them nonetheless. The same applies to work tasks. Integration of these tasks into your daily timeline simply means that they are all completed at an appropriate point. It becomes less about what time of day they are completed and more about ensuring that they have been completed.

Having freed yourself from a time-constrained day, you become more imaginative about how and when to do tasks. If you share your life with others in a domestic situation, your flexibility will be tailored to suit all of you. You are probably not going to win any popularity prizes with your family if you decide that 2 a.m. is the best time of the day for you to vacuum your house. However, deciding that you will start work-related tasks at 6 a.m. instead of 8 a.m. may well have less of an impact on others around you and provide you with the opportunity to add more pleasure-related tasks to your day.

What might your day look like if you planned it out with less of a focus on a Monday-to-Friday, 8 a.m.-to-6 p.m. pattern and more of an open agenda? Being deliberate about integrating all the tasks you need to complete in a day ensures that not only do the tasks get completed but also that you have the opportunity to enjoy the Out of Office work style. For example, in talking with some people who are home based, I found that many had not considered taking their work-related tasks to alternate locations, unless they were meeting with someone. Taking a laptop to the park and completing work tasks there, followed by a walk, integrates exercise, relaxation, and work into one section of the day. Without planning that, though, it is all too easy to simply stay home, work during the day, and perhaps run to the store and grab some groceries, and then return home to complete more work tasks.

That isn't really integration; it is still the segmentation that we are used to and to some extent trained to do. Those who are new to the Out of Office work style often feel guilty about having the freedom to integrate what was previously thought of as work into their whole life. They think in terms of themselves as being away from the office but still tied to it and the conventions it requires. Integration allows them to not feel that guilt, but there is a shift in thinking required before that freedom from guilt can happen.

Does your manager, boss, or client care that you completed a work task in the park and then went for a walk? No, in my experience, when it comes to remote workers, all anyone really cares about is that the work product is completed when needed. They prefer a "black box" approach. That is, they aren't really interested in how something happens; they are more interested in the fact that it happens when it is needed.

Stop Conforming

If those managing us are truly not as interested in how the work is completed as much they are that it is completed, then, with a few exceptions, we are free to manage our days as we wish. Yet, many of us still conform to our old lifestyle. I believe this is mostly because we haven't considered or been shown an alternative. The integration lifestyle is that alternative. I encourage you to stop trying to achieve a balance between work and life and instead embrace the idea that you can, in fact, successfully integrate the two into a whole life perspective that enables you to still complete tasks as needed but with much less stress and anxiety and with more freedom and a sense of control.

If you are trusted, either by your organization or yourself, to be working Out of Office, then surely you are trusted enough to plan your days appropriately and still have the freedom to enjoy your time. How many hours have you wasted worrying about tasks that you didn't complete because you traded that time for something else? A little discipline and forethought goes a long way in ensuring that you have time for everything and that the things that matter get done.

I can almost hear some of you reading this now saying that I obviously don't work for your boss, your clients, or in your industry. Well, of course I don't. I don't know your life, or how you organize it. What I *do* know is that an increasing number of people are taking on the Out of Office work style but are doing so in a manner that means they are simply swapping locations and not changing the mindset that they bring with them.

This means that both they and the people they work with and for do not fully experience the benefits of this type of working. There are so many more benefits than simply being able to meet your child from the bus stop at the end of the school day or being able to pick up the groceries in the morning when the store is less busy. One of the biggest benefits I have seen among my peers is that once they have untethered themselves from a restricted way of approaching the Out of Office work style, their creativity increases. Because they are looking at a major part of their lives in a different manner, they start to look at other things with a different perspective.

The solutions that they create are different, more imaginative, sometimes more daring than those they previously had. After all, if you start thinking differently about something as major as how you spend your day, then surely it is reasonable to imagine you will apply that thinking to everything you tackle. Better solutions and more imaginative thinking benefits everyone; clients, organizations, co-workers all get to benefit from this different way of examining issues. Again, this should be part of the process when considering Out of Office working. Does the person, do you as an individual, feel capable of changing the way you approach tasks, the way you approach life?

For those who lack the flexibility of making a major change in their perspective, working Out of Office is most likely to remain simply a change in location and not really bring the full benefits of the work style with it. It becomes more about convenience, perhaps cost savings, and other considerations. This is where you then see team fragmentation, isolation, and a decline in productivity occur. Working Out of Office isn't just a different way of working; it is a different way of thinking, a different way of considering what work, life, and time mean to a person. By accepting that the change of location is less important than the change of thinking, a person and the organization they are attached to become able to fully realize the benefits available to them from Out of Office working.

Applying this criteria, the ability to change an ingrained way of thinking of how work and life integrate can change the way in which an organization decides to select or even implement Out of Office working. First, change is hard—for both individuals and organizations. As I have already discussed in previous chapters, the most likely candidates for Out of Office working are likely to be more experienced workers, those who understand both the industry they work in and, if appropriate, the organization they work for. However, this also means that they are likely to have spent more time in the traditional, in-office environment and therefore have taken on the more traditional way of perceiving work and life. The question that needs to be asked is, can they change?

Just as importantly, can the organization change where necessary to accommodate the shift in thinking that the employees will bring who are working Out of Office. It is one thing to imagine that you want more creative thinking and more creative solutions within the organization, but is the organization ready to embrace them, to implement them, and can they be integrated with the way others who are still based in-office think? Just to clarify, here, I am not suggesting that those who are working in-office lack imagination or creativity. I am simply highlighting that when you encourage one group of people to start thinking differently than another group, it can become a point of conflict.

I encourage you to think about how you have spent your past few days: How did you allocate your tasks? Was it based on an exchange of time? Was it based on a prioritization based on money? Was it based on how those tasks fit best into your life?

If you aren't happy with the way you have allocated your tasks, think about changing the way you do things. I am not providing a "blueprint" for happiness, or how your individual day should look. Only you can do that. Only you know your situation and the tasks that face you each day. I do really believe, however, that with a little creative thinking and the readiness to change how you view your tasks, you can achieve a much greater level of integration than you currently have.

I encourage you to stop trying to achieve a value-based balance in your life and instead integrate your whole life so that you can achieve more, do more, and experience more of the benefits of working Out of Office.

9

Time to Go Back to the Office

For some people, working Out of Office is a temporary situation. Perhaps they are between jobs, or between locations. For others there simply comes a point in their life where they want to return to the office. Perhaps it is a work opportunity that is too good to say no to; perhaps it is something more mercenary like the need for health insurance. Whatever the reason, it is important to recognize when that point is reached—if for no other reason than continuing to work in an environment that you no longer enjoy will negatively impact you on many fronts, including personal, professional, mental, and physical health.

The transition back to the in-office work style is not easy, nor is it usually straightforward. Just as the transition to the Out of Office work style needs careful thought and planning, so too does the transition in the opposite direction.

From commuting routes and culture changes, to simple things such as deciding whether you are going to take a lunch or find somewhere near the office to eat. All these things need to be given some level of consideration. Perhaps more important is the impact it will have on others. How will those at home make the transition? Children, pets, and partners all need to make the transition with you.

If you have been working from home, for example, perhaps one of the tasks you completed was to collect the children from school. Will they now ride the school bus? Will your partner collect them or will you have to make some other arrangement? Pets are particular sensitive to change. When I am at home for long periods, our cats get into a very set routine of where they sleep and when they want attention from me. If I am gone during the day on consecutive days, it disturbs them greatly and their routine changes dramatically when I return. I can only imagine the disruption it would cause if I were to transition back to working in an office away from home on a full-time basis.

Of course, all of these things can be overcome, worked around, and compensated for; however, it would be foolish to simply pretend that they don't exist and to not factor them into your planning. The more thought you give these and other considerations, the easier the transition becomes on those around you, which of course makes the transition easier on you.

How can you tell it is time for you to return to the office? A lot of the reasons are simply the same as the ones I discussed in Chapter 1, "Why You Shouldn't Try an Out of Office Experience." You miss being around co-workers and having the social exchanges. You want more space or your work has evolved to a point where you need more professional surroundings for clients. Perhaps the nature of the work you do has changed and it has become impractical for you to continue working remotely.

For some people, the transition back to the in-office work style comes as part of a promotion. For others, it is the decision to join a larger organization and to discontinue operating their own business that prompts the transition. Some organizations, while seemingly embracing the Out of Office work style, are not yet comfortable with senior positions being filled by remote workers. I'm not quite sure what message this sends to employees—whether these organizations feel that senior managers need to have a presence in the main community to enable them to exert an influence on the employees they manage or if they feel that having a senior manager working Out of Office will make them somehow less accessible.

I have known some organizations that have enabled senior managers to work Out of Office and have not suffered for it, but the majority of businesses are still in a period of conversion. Many organizations are still wary of this type of work style and are not convinced of the benefits it holds. Other organizations have removed this type of working from their environment, as Yahoo! did in 2013, for operational reasons. This is a different type of transition, one where the employee is not making the decision but rather is being told that they must work from an office under the control of the organization. I can see many issues with this type of transition, even if it is handled in an empathetic manner.

All the issues I discussed earlier in this chapter exist in this situation, but they may be compounded by resentment, feelings of distrust toward managers, a sense that control has been lost or revoked, and an impression that they as an individual employee are not trusted. Although none of these may in fact be the reason for the transition, the fact that they may enter the psyche of the workers affected must be addressed to ensure a successful transition from one work style to another.

Many organizations have experience with this type of transition in other forms— for example, assisting women who are returning to the workplace after an absence while caring for children. Other organizations have experience in employing military veterans who have been working in a different type of Out of Office work style. There may well be a lot of similarities in handling these transitions that an organization can leverage in helping those returning from the Out of Office work style. The important thing for organizations to recognize is that those returning to an in-office environment bring with them a different perspective on achieving goals than those who have maintained an in-office work style consistently. That is not to say one is better than the other, but certainly there will be a difference in the way solutions are arrived at.

When working Out of Office, an employee will have had a greater sense of freedom, and there may well have been fewer adherences to a strict workday. If a person was self-employed previously, they may well have a strong sense of solving problems in isolation rather than within a team framework. These are all considerations that have to be examined when an organization decides to bring employees back to the in-office work style.

Likewise, these are also considerations for the individual. Yes, perhaps you have become isolated, and you miss the easy banter that having a team around you brings. You miss brainstorming solutions with other smart people, or you miss the support systems that tend to come with larger organizations. But are you ready to give up control to others? If you have been running your own business and making all the decisions, do you consider yourself ready to have some if not all of those decisions made for you?

Whereas you may have had budgetary control over your business, you may not within an organization. If you decided who was hired and who was fired in your own business, that may not be your responsibility in your new role. Of course, these are all things you are going to consider before accepting an offer, but in the excitement of examining the benefits of returning to a larger organization, it can be easy to overlook the things that drew you to the Out of Office work style in the first place.

The Out of Office work style may have lost some of its appeal for you, but is it just one aspect of the work style that is prompting you to make a change or the whole experience? The lure of something different, something that seems to require less effort, perhaps, can be all too attractive. Making the transition back to an in-office environment is not quite as easily undone as making the transition to the Out of Office work style.

Remember that first day at a new school? How everything seemed so large, how everyone else seemed to know the rules, where to be, and how and when to get there? That has always struck me as the same experience when joining a new organization. It can take weeks, sometimes longer to learn the structure, politics, and the rhythm of an organization.

Of course, these are not reasons not to make the transition; they are simply concepts that need to be considered carefully before making the transition.

For many, the transition is relatively painless, and there comes with it a whole host of associated benefits: the reconnection with co-workers in a shared physical space, the making of new acquaintances in a new workplace, the opportunity to learn new skills or extend existing ones, the regularity of in-office hours, and the chance to have a clearer demarcation of the start and end of the workday.

All these elements can contribute to both the desire for the return to an in-office work style and the sense of relief for some people when they return to this style of working. I have considered the return myself many times over the years; for all of the aforementioned reasons as well as the opportunity to work with smart people, to have a space that is dedicated to my work, and so on. However, I have always realized in the end that I am better suited to working Out of Office, and if I were indeed to return to the in-office work style, I wouldn't enjoy the transition or the routine.

The other reason is that like many solopreneurs, I enjoy a multiple income stream lifestyle. That is to say, I work more than one job! I am a writer, a photographer, and a speaker as well as being a consultant. In any one day I might be working all or several of these jobs. The variety in my day is something that keeps me energized. That is a luxury that most in-office workers do not get to enjoy; rather, they are mission focused on one set of outcomes. Even if they achieve this through multiple projects, the work itself is, at its core, the same.

However, this sense of focus and purpose is yet another reason why many return to the fold of a more formal organizational setting and enjoy the transition back to the in-office work style. The sense that they are able to dedicate eight or nine hours a day to one aim and do so without the pulls and distractions that home life can often provide is something that they enjoy. In addition, the impromptu meetings, the hallway conversations, and the casual comments that accompany interacting with a team of co-workers only add to the enjoyment of the in-office environment.

As Steven MacDonald shared with me:

> *I was working from home for more than a year and recently got back into an office environment. One of the main reasons why I preferred an office environment to working from home is the fact I can be around real people and not just spend my day talking through Skype or IM. Information shared during coffee breaks or standing by the water cooler is priceless.*
>
> *Working from home in short doses is great—one day per week or a few days per month, but the "glamour" of working from home wears off quickly.*

Steven makes an interesting point about the "glamour" of working from home wearing off. At its core, this statement sums up how a lot of people I spoke to felt about why they would transition back to the in-office work style. Steven also identifies the feeling of dislocation that technology can produce. Yes, it's amazing that we can have "face-to-face" meetings with people who may be thousands of miles away through technology such as Skype, but the sense of being around people is missing. Think about any meetings you have attended in an office environment. There are usually three parts to a meeting. First is the arrival, which is where people catch up, ask how your weekend was or how your recent business trip went, and maybe ask about another project you are working on together. Then there is the meeting itself, and finally there is the departure, when you perhaps walk with someone to their cube or grab a coffee on the way back to your respective desks. During this time, further conversation ensues, perhaps about the meeting or perhaps about other topics. With a videoconference, the arrival portion is usually kept fairly brief; the bulk of the time is focused on the topic of the meeting, and of course there is no departure section other than hanging up the call.

So although technology allows you to get the job done, it doesn't allow for all those nuanced interactions we as human beings enjoy so much. Email has a tendency to be even more focused, lacking the nonverbal cues that allow us to take a conversation in different directions or to assess someone's real reaction to information. Although instant messaging is a little more conversational, and the use of emoticons can help put a message into some type of context, it is still no real replacement for in-person communication.

Face-to-face communication is also a lot faster. Emails can be ignored, lost, or lead to endless chains. Phone or video calls are the next best thing, but as human beings, we are wired to communicate in the presence of each other, so we are able to convey a lot more information when we are with the other people we are trying to communicate with. I have had brainstorming sessions via telephone and videoconference, and although they are successful I often wonder what the outcome might have been if we had the opportunity to put that same group of people in a room together and allow the cross-conversations that often occur in a face-to-face setting that are often missing from phone and video calls. My instinct tells me that although the ultimate solution might look similar, the path that was taken to reach it might well have been quite different and produced some other interesting ideas that the phone and video calls did not.

For some, the transition back to an in-office work style is prompted by a change of life style at home. Lidia Varesco Racoma shared her story with me about the way the birth of her son changed how she worked, forcing a transition from a home-based office to renting a formal office space:

> I made the switch to an office last year, after 11 years of working from home. Or should I say, I got kicked out: After my son was born, I had to relocate my home office to make space for the baby nursery.
>
> It was quite a change, having worked from home for so long. But what I enjoy most is being able to fully focus on work, without home-based distractions (laundry, dishes, etc.). I like also like having the space to store reference and art materials required for my job as a graphic designer, as well as inventory (I launched a baby and kids apparel business earlier this year). Having an office has also provided opportunity to network with fellow small business owners (a fellow business in my office building even hired me for a project). It's nice to be able to "unplug" when I'm at home. Though I have a laptop, there is less inclination to work when I'm at home. Of course, having a toddler running around makes that impossible anyway!

Even though Lidia continued to work for herself, she felt that the lack of room and the ability to clearly differentiate between home and work spaces helped her business. As she mentioned, having proximity to other small businesses helped her generate new business. For Lidia, the move was not only about making room for her business outside the home but also about seeing her business differently. What I found most interesting about Lidia's story was that fact that having moved into an office she felt less tempted to work when at home and therefore her focus is on her child and home life rather than seeking to integrate the two.

Being able to turn off from work can be a very cathartic process for many people and allows them to return to their work more refreshed than when work is a constant. In much the same way as a vacation can allow you to feel re-energized, for some people, simply being able to shut the door on an office at the end of each day can lead to the same feelings, albeit on a smaller scale. This ability to leave work at "work" and switch off, or as Lidia phrased it "unplug," is one of the advantages that recurred often in my conversations with people about why they returned to an in-office environment.

If you remember back to Chapter 1, you'll start to see a familiar pattern forming here with the reasons why a person might want to return to an in-office environment. In fact, many of the reasons people gave for not embracing the Out of Office work style are in fact the same reasons why they returned to the in-office work style—perhaps rather unsurprisingly so.

What this really tells me is that the reasons I explored in Chapter 1 are valid as both reasons not to commit to the Out of Office work style in the first place and reasons why some people eventually transition back to the in-office work style. It also highlights that although certain people are better suited to the Out of Office work style than others, there are some who can make it work for short periods of time before they need to return to the in-office environment.

This poses an interesting option for employers. Can they devise a work style that takes advantage of both methods of working? Would it be possible from an organizational perspective to have employees who work part of the year Out of Office and part of the year in-office? For example, would parents enjoy the opportunity to work Out of Office during the summer vacation, returning to the in-office work style when school commences? Could an organization adapt to that type of flexible work force?

Could a blended work style replace the more formal vacation days? Would employees be willing to trade vacation days as they currently understand them for longer periods where they are free to work Out of Office? If vacation days were traded for the Out of Office work style, would it invite employees to view the time away from a formal office setting as their own time? The Out of Office work style poses many questions for employer and employee alike, and much depends on the willingness of both to make changes to how they perceive employment. When I think about the employment contracts I have both written and signed over my career working for organizations, a lot of the clauses reference time spent on company tasks. Certain clauses reference copyright and ownership of intellectual property; they refer to ideas and concepts that are created while on company time and engaged in company work. How relevant are these clauses to individuals who are integrating their work and home life? How does an organization clearly delineate a time when "thinking" was classified as work time if the person was working Out of Office and had the idea while walking their dog?

I'm not going to try and solve those puzzles in these pages; they are for much bigger conversations among much smarter people than me. What these questions tell me is that before we see a broader adoption of the Out of Office work style, we are going to have to see a much broader change in the way we classify, think about, and relate to work—at least certain categories of work.

For some Out of Office workers, the transition to in-office working doesn't necessarily mean joining an organization or even renting their own office space. For some, it is the transition from working alone, perhaps at home, to working in a more communal environment. The impacts on how someone works when they transition from working alone to working in a communal space are often similar to those seen among the Out of Office worker transitioning to a formal in-office setting.

Adrienne Capollupo shared her story of moving from working at home to joining a co-working space and the impact it had on her and her business. The intriguing nature of co-working spaces is that they are neither completely Out of Office nor completely in-office, offering as they do, some of the benefits and downsides of both:

> *I previously worked from home, and while the benefits were great, I missed having co-workers, plus I was distracted by my children. After looking at many options for office space, I decided to join a co-working space. The concept was brand new in our town and is starting to catch on. When I joined the space, I was employed in a telecommuting role for sales and marketing at a software company. After joining the co-working space, Roanoke Business Lounge, I met small business owners and found a niche that my skill set could fill. So, I resigned from my employer and started a successful company. Making the move from working from home to co-working gave me the opportunity to launch a business while filling my need for interaction with others on a professional level.*

I found Adrienne's story interesting on a couple levels. As we have heard from several others who shared their stories about Out of Office working from home, domestic situations can become very distracting. Children can impact the effectiveness and productivity of those working from home quite suddenly. I doubt I know any parent who would rather perform work tasks over providing care and attention to their sick child. Obviously and quite rightly (in my opinion) children come first. However, the employee has to make up that workload at some point, and that can be very stressful.

What really struck me was that Adrienne initially sought an office space where she could be more effective in her role for the company that she worked for, but in solving her issues of missing the interaction with co-workers and removing the distractions of children, she discovered an opportunity to work for herself. We've seen how the Out of Office work style can lead to people exploring their entrepreneurial abilities in previous chapters—whether they are working from a co-working space traveling for business as a lone woman or finding it hard to locate food that fits their dietary requirements while on the road.

This ability to turn a situation of working Out of Office into a business opportunity is one example of what I am referring to when I talk about the different way in which the employees best suited to this work style think. The challenge for an organization with these types of employees is retaining them by giving them both the opportunity to utilize their creative type of thinking in their role and providing them enough challenges that they maintain an interest in continuing to work for the organization. Quite obviously in the situations I've already shown, that wasn't the case, and the organizations lost out to the opportunity that the individual discovered on their own. That is not to say that these individuals would not have gone on to build their own companies anyway, but an organization that truly values these individuals makes it a much harder choice to leave.

The issue of employee retention is certainly a consideration for any organization that provides an Out of Office environment for certain employees. As I mentioned in Chapter 1, it takes a particular set of skills for an employee to be considered for this work style, and those skills are also what makes those employees both attractive to other organizations and increases the likelihood that they will have entrepreneurial thoughts and desires of their own.

With this in mind, I can understand why some organizations are reticent to introduce the Out of Office work style. Hiring, training, and equipping employees are major cost centers in any organization. Losing employees, like losing customers, involves a cost to any organization. Better to retain an employee than to have to replace them. However, with the Out of Office work style, retention has a different set of challenges. These types of employees are trusted to be able to work without constant supervision; they are relied upon to be able to produce effectively and to meet and in many cases exceed expectations. At the same time, these traits are all ones that make the employee attractive to competitors. It is much easier for an Out of Office worker to meet with a recruiter or potential new employer than it is for their in-office counterpart. It is much easier for them to hide the fact that they might in fact be looking for a new role outside the organization.

This means that anyone managing this type of worker needs to be more than just a regular manager; they need to be able to pick up on the small nuances in conversations via phone or video, to read between the lines in emails, and to assess changes that are communicated in abstract ways by Out of Office workers. The implication of this is that not only does an organization need particular skills in the employees it selects as suitable to work Out of Office, but it needs a particular skill set in the employees it selects to manage those working Out of Office.

For smaller organizations, this is a lot to ask. If your company only employs 50 people, what are the chances that you have both a group of individuals who have the skill set to work Out of Office and a second group that have the skill set to manage them?

Even in large organizations, this type of selection process will not be easy. From the examples I have seen, many organizations don't consider this second layer and ignore the implications that they are sending some of their most skilled people out into an environment where they not only have more freedom but are being actively encouraged to explore that freedom.

The essential message here is that any organization that wants to have a successful set of Out of Office workers needs to provide a support structure that goes with that work style. In addition, the organization also needs to provide a method of successfully transitioning those workers back into the in-office work style when the time is right.

With the right leaders, it should be possible to identify the moment when an Out of Office worker is ready for that transition and work with them to create both an atmosphere where the worker feels comfortable in making the transition and an environment where that conversation can be held effectively.

The attractions of working Out of Office, which I have covered at length in previous chapters, are also listed as reasons why someone would want to return to the in-office environment. Two sides of the same coin perhaps? Where one person finds a benefit and another finds a detriment, is what we are seeing really just the personality types found in any organization? Or are we seeing a change in the way people view how they work?

I tend to think that we are seeing the latter. In other words, as we as a society evolve, these new work styles appear and are embraced as alternatives, only to be rejected by some because they don't provide the opportunity that those early adopters thought they would. This doesn't invalidate the work style, nor does it mean that those individuals were unsuited to the work style. Rather, I believe it indicates that the work style has not yet reached a maturation point where it is suited to as broad a range of individuals as it eventually will be.

We heard from Kim Miller in Chapter 3, "The Challenges," when we discussed the way some organizations and individuals don't yet regard Out of Office working as a serious option. Kim went on to share that she was moving back to an in-office environment as her business grew. Remember from Kim's story in Chapter 3 the job applicant who brought a neighbor with them for "protection"? I'm sure that part of her experience of moving to a formal office space will be to find that applicants no longer show up with neighbors to interview with her!

> ...fast forward 15 months and I have just signed a lease on an office space. As wonderful as it is to wear flip flops to my desk, I have found the barking dogs and the cleaning lady's vacuum to be too much for me to handle. Soon I will be back in more business-appropriate attire and absorbing an office expense of several thousand dollars a month. But I will have an office without an overprotective barking dog, the cleaning crew will mop when no one is working, and I will be able to walk across the street for a cup of coffee instead of reaching for my keys for a drive down the road.

As Kim shows, it isn't just the distractions at home that can prompt people to move to an in-office environment; the success of their business and the need to hire additional workers, workers who themselves are not willing or ready to take on the Out of Office work style, can be a factor in why someone might move to an in-office environment. For some, like Kim, this was an acceptable trade; for others it can be seen as part of the cost of success.

I think it is important to note here that transitioning back to in-office is not a sign that you have failed at working Out of Office. There are a number of reasons why someone might choose to make that transition. It is equally important to note that the transition to an in-office environment doesn't necessarily mean someone is giving up their own business to work for someone else. As we have seen from Kim's story, her transition was part of growing her business.

Sheila Kale shared an interesting set of thoughts about the separation of work and home life. For her, the enjoyment of working in an office comes from the fact that she feels empowered to enjoy her time away from the office. For Sheila, there were definite advantages to working in a more formal in-office environment:

> An office separates work time from family and leisure time. I found gardening, cooking, and cleaning easily distracted me. Having an office helped me set boundaries. An office helps define work time for friends and family. When you work from home, people tend to think you are always available. An office is a statement that I am serious about my new career. I enjoy unshared space designed just to create and to connect

with my clients. I love the freedom of knowing I have given my time to work I love, now I have time for fun, family, community, and hobbies.

For two years I worked at home as I developed a coaching business. Something always grabbed my attention away from the work I was doing. Since I had so many distractions, I tried to make up the time by using my evenings. There were no boundaries. Having a dedicated space to work gave me freedom to enjoy time away from work.

This theme of separating work and home continues to return to the conversations I have with individuals and organizations about how the Out of Office work style might or might not be implemented for them. As I discussed in Chapter 8, "Work/ Life Integration," I believe that integration is the key—rather than trying to balance the two. I think that for as long as people try to achieve a balance between the two elements of their lives, they will struggle and eventually find ways in which to build clear boundaries between them.

I find this disheartening, especially for those who work for themselves. If any group of individuals should display an enjoyment and passion for what they do to generate income, it should be those who work for themselves, who are expressing their own entrepreneurial spirit. But if those individuals find themselves having to build boundaries between work and life, I really think they are viewing these two elements incorrectly. I also see it as part of the path back to the in-office environment, which for many means either sacrificing the freedom that they thought they were going to gain by working for themselves or sacrificing what they were working for in order to return to a larger organization.

Either way, I believe in that situation that they have lost. That is not to say I believe that working in an office environment is a negative experience or that only those who have given up on bigger dreams do so. Lots of individuals who have extremely successful careers enjoy the in-office environment immensely. The sense of group, of team, of being able to mentor and to learn from those around them—these are all important factors for these particular individuals and for many like them.

I do believe that for as long as we continue to try to see work and life as two separate elements of our existence, we will continue to see people dip in and out of the Out of Office work style. Perhaps our struggle to balance the two says more about our view of how work defines who we are as individuals than it does about how we want to work. Think about the last social gathering you were at; think about those opening moments when you met someone new for the first time. What were the first few questions you asked them and they in turn asked you? I would wager that "What do you do?" was among them.

"What do you do?" is such an innocuous phrase and is actually without meaning if taken as just a question. But we immediately interpret it as "What do you do to earn money?," "What do you do to contribute to society?," or "What do you to validate who you are?."

All those implied questions sitting among those four words. In fact, we are often asked what we do for work before we are asked about our other activities. It helps us define who we are talking to, how we compare to that other person, and whether we perceive ourselves as more or less successful as they are. I've noticed an interesting reaction when I respond to that question with something vague like "I'm in marketing." The follow up is "Where do you work?" The implication is, "Do you work for an organization?" When I respond, "I work from home," there is an immediate reaction—sometimes positive, sometimes negative.

The reaction is very similar to the reaction I used to get when I told people I was a vegetarian. Some wanted to challenge the validity of that choice; others wanted to apologize for their own meat-eating preferences. So it goes with the conversation about working the Out of Office work style. Some will ask how on earth you get anything done; others will confirm that it is something they have always wanted to try but aren't sure they are the right "type."

If you are currently working the Out of Office work style, take the self-assessment at the end of Chapter 1 and see if you are still most likely to be suited to the work style now that you have been doing it for a while. If you aren't, then perhaps it's time for you to return to an in-office environment or perhaps it's time for you to assess how you are integrating work and life.

I think that many of the people I spoke to while writing this book who moved back to the in-office setting did so, in part at least, because they grew tired of trying to balance work and life. I'm really not surprised at this; it is an exhausting activity, which is why I am such a proponent of integration rather than balance.

If you are considering moving back to the in-office environment, I'd encourage you to reread Chapter 8 and take a look at how successful you have been so far at moving toward an integrated lifestyle before making that decision. Of course, if the decision is based less on not being able to balance work and life and is more about an opportunity, that won't be as relevant. Still, even for those working solely from an in-office environment I think the exercise of finding ways to integrate the two elements has a positive effect.

All of us are becoming more connected, more integrated into a whole lifestyle where work and leisure blur. Accepting that balance is no longer really achievable, but integration can reduce stress and help lessen guilt about not having balanced work and life at the end of each week.

Planning for the next way of working (which is for many already here) allows an individual to acquire new skills and retain relevance in the workplace. I have encountered individuals who are extremely resistant to the new work style. They refuse to take home laptops or other devices from the office in the evenings or during weekends and are therefore incommunicado. Although these individuals feel that they are making a statement about what they perceive as their "free time," the statement they are really making is that they are unwilling to blend work and leisure and that they want a clearly black-and-white world. In a world that is increasingly lived in shades of gray, is that really the message you want to send?

©CasaWeenie.com 2013

10

Tools and Tech to Help

There are literally hundreds of tools and technology to help you in your quest to be more efficient and enjoy the Out of Office work style. I'm not going to try and list them all, but I do want to suggest a few. Some you may already be familiar with, and some may be completely new to you.

Many of these tools I have either tried or am a regular user of. Some of them I don't use simply because my type of work doesn't call for them, but I have received recommendations for them from others.

As with any tool, simply having it won't make you more efficient or allow you to increase your productivity. Utilizing the tools as needed and learning what they can do for you is at the core of being successful with them. Having a set of wrenches in your garage doesn't make you a master mechanic. So downloading apps or signing up for services won't actually help unless you are prepared to put in some effort to learn the tool and find out how it fits into your workflow.

Where possible, I have listed tools that are compatible with the most popular operating systems. I have tried to avoid any that only run on a specific phone or computer. If there is a tool that is specific to a particular operating system, I have indicated that.

I've organized the following chapter into sections that are based around the types of tools and technology so that you can quickly refer to them as you start to explore which of the tools will be of most help to you.

As with the other products mentioned in this book, none of the products listed are endorsements, and I have no connection with any company or organization offering them. I am listing them because I (or friends) have used them and found them to be of help in the Out of Office work style.

Videoconferencing

I'm starting with videoconferencing because it has become such an important tool for so many Out of Office workers. What I like about the current generation of tools in this space is that they are just as useful for staying in touch with work colleagues as they are for staying in touch with personal contacts.

Skype

One of the most popular of the videoconferencing tools, Skype has a range of features that covers most users' requirements. Although it starts off as a free service, the most useful parts of the service do require the user to pay.

Figure 10.1 shows a multiuser video call, which is not part of the free service but is certainly a worthwhile feature to pay for. Given that this capability was restricted to large corporate offices only a few years ago, it shows just how far the technology has come.

Figure 10.1   *Skype (credit Skype, used with permission)*

Skype is not restricted to just the computer environment and works well on cell phones as well. Although its video calling feature is perhaps its most well known, it can also be used for voice calling, including calls to international numbers, cell phones, and landlines.

This makes it an incredible useful communication tool for any sized organization. Given the charges that cellular carriers levy on their subscribers for international use of cell phones, Skype's fees are extremely reasonable for anyone traveling and needing to make calls back to their home country. The only caveat is that you must have a Wi-Fi connection that has a reasonable bandwidth. Public Wi-Fi is not always reliable in all areas and sometimes only hotels or corporate environments will offer the type of bandwidth needed to make a good video call. However, voice calls require less bandwidth, and of course not everyone has access to a device where video would be available.

Calling a colleague's cell phone or an office landline becomes a lot less expensive and more realistic when you are in control of the cost rather than at the mercy of a cellular roaming charge.

The cheapest way to use Skype is to call another Skype user—those calls are free. So getting your team all on the same system is definitely an advantage, and once you have decided that Skype (or another system) is going to be the communication tool you favor, it only makes sense to leverage this type of cost-saving feature.

The Skype-to-Skype free calling feature works both internationally and within countries. The calls are also unlimited in terms of length, so if you want a long call home, for free, this is definitely a system for you to consider.

Another feature that Skype has is instant messaging, for those quick questions; an instant message is like having free text messaging on your device. This feature works from phones and computers and is again free to use. It also integrates with Facebook contacts so you can send messages from Skype to Facebook friends via the Facebook messenger system.

One of the features I find most useful when using Skype is the ability to share my screen. I can walk a client through a piece of software, a concept, or anything else on my computer without having to email them a document or link. This means they can focus on what I am showing them and less on the file they have received.

FaceTime

FaceTime is only available to users of Apple's operating systems for phone and computers. This application, which works on any of Apple's current devices, allows for free video calls between two users (see Figure 10.2).

Figure 10.2 *FaceTime (credit Apple Inc., used with permission)*

Although the fact that the call can only involve two users limits this app's appeal for business users, it is undeniable that the clarity and reliability of the app for videoconferencing makes it very appealing to those looking for a simple solution. It is also limited by the fact that it only works on Apple devices, which for many is a major drawback, given the higher price point of these devices. However, because it works equally well from an iPhone or iPad, the cost becomes less of a consideration. Again, I highly recommend making sure you are on a high-bandwidth Wi-Fi connection before using this app. It does work on 4G networks very well, but unless you are on an unlimited data plan, you will find yourself using your data allowance very quickly if you make a lot of FaceTime calls. There are no additional features with this application. It does one thing, but it does it very well.

I personally think of this as more of a personal communication tool than a business one. However, at least for small businesses, it has some usefulness. The fact that it is more or less a one-touch tool that allows instant videoconferencing makes it appealing to even the most technically challenged users.

Google Hangout

The Google+ social networking platform offers the ability for up to ten people to videoconference together at the same time via its Hangout feature (see Figure 10.3). What's more, the service is free.

This feature has become one of the most popular parts of Google's social network and is used by a variety of organizations for both public and private videoconferencing. It has even been used by President Obama to answer questions from ordinary members of the public.

Figure 10.3 *Google Hangout (credit Google Inc., used with permission)*

There are no geographic restrictions to the service, as long as the participants have a good Internet connection and a webcam, they can join the conference. The only other requirement is that they have a Google account. Participants can also instant message one another and even mute a participant, in addition to muting their own audio and hiding their video. Thus, if one of the conference participants has a noisy background that is distracting, they can mute their sound until they need to speak.

Overall the service is easy to use, quick to learn, and makes videoconferencing for groups achievable without cost. Any distributed team would benefit from using this service.

In addition to general hangouts, there are also Hangouts On Air. These are currently only allowed as public sessions but do benefit from the fact that they can be recorded and uploaded to a YouTube channel. Once they have been uploaded to YouTube (an automated process that takes approximately 24 hours), videos can be marked as private to provide some privacy in the event something proprietary is being discussed. Hangouts On Air are also free.

Given the volume of videos on YouTube and the number of Hangouts On Air, it is fairly unlikely that a random user would find your meeting particularly interesting. I think this has the potential to replace minutes of meetings and allow for meetings to be distributed easily and freely to employees who were not able to attend.

GoToMeeting

GoToMeeting is a product from Citrix Online (see Figure 10.4). It is more than just a videoconferencing tool, but I have included it in this section because that is the feature most people are probably familiar with. As a videoconferencing tool, it is feature rich. Users are shown in high definition (where available), providing extremely high-quality video images, which makes for a less distracting call than one where all you can see is the vague impression of someone whose image is very pixelated.

Figure 10.4   *GoToMeeting (credit Citrix Systems, used with permission)*

GoToMeeting also optimizes the experience for each user on the call, making the necessary adjustments depending on the device and available bandwidth that each user has. This also helps produce a less distracting environment.

All these features are available on mobile devices as well and, similar to Skype, are operating system independent. Where GoToMeeting excels beyond just videoconferencing is in the collaboration space. The person initiating the call not only can share their screen but also can hand over control of their mouse and keyboard to another user during the call.

I have used GoToMeeting as a co-presenter in online webinars. Being able to advance your own slides during your presentation, even though they are on someone else's device, and not having to resort to the "next slide" phrase at the end of each slide is a very freeing experience as a presenter. GoToMeeting also lends itself to large-scale collaborations because not only can users join the session from a smartphone or computer, they can also simply dial in to a session from a regular phone in the same way they would for an audio conference.

By not restricting the way users can participate, the level of engagement is much higher. My view of technology has always been that it should be transparent—that is to say it should not get in the way of the objective. I would have to say that

GoToMeeting is very good at getting out of the way of the session and the users and simply acting as a facilitation tool.

Gadgets

A new gadget seems to hit the shelves on a weekly (if not daily) basis. In this section, I have gathered a couple that have been around for a while and that I have been using and can attest to their ability to make working Out of Office a little easier.

Neat Receipts

One of the biggest challenges that Out of Office workers who travel have is keeping up with receipts. I personally find it a chore to remember to collect them all, and then when I get home to remember to file them and allocate them to the trip I just took.

To try and cut down on the amount of time I was spending tackling that particular chore, I invested in a Neat Receipts scanner (see Figure 10.5). Basically it is a portable document scanner that I can carry with me when I am on the road to scan and file my receipts electronically, putting them in a folder that I have designated on my computer. That way, if I lose a receipt while I am traveling, I have an electronic copy of it already filed.

Figure 10.5 *Neat Receipts (credit The Neat Company, used with permission)*

What I really like about this system is that the software learns what type of documents you are scanning and where it should file them. So if I want to scan a group of documents that are different, it can cope with that without a lot of input from me. For example, I might be scanning a business card, followed by a meal receipt, followed by a page from a notebook; all very different documents that all need to be filed in different ways.

I particularly like the way it handles receipts; it groups them by vendor or by other data elements, such as date. Grouping by vendor allows you to see at a glance how much you have spent with a particular vendor. So, for example, if you want to know just how much you spent in Starbucks on that last business trip, you can do so with just a mouse click—but be careful, the result of that can be shocking for some!

The software allows you to change a category of document that you have scanned and redesignates the scan. The device itself fits into a briefcase or laptop bag and doesn't need power cable; it runs from the USB port on your computer, which makes it ideal for international travel as well as domestic.

Overall I have found this to be the best of the scanning solutions available, and that includes the scanning apps available on smartphones that just don't seem to be as able to cope with documents the way the Neat Receipt does. Neat Receipts is available for both PC and Mac.

Mophie Phone Case

One of the most annoying things about our dependency on our smartphones is that we are dependent on them! The lengths that we will go to ensure that we stay connected are amazing. As I mentioned in an earlier chapter, I have watched and participated in the act of being a power vulture, hovering by an outlet so that as soon as it becomes available I can plug in my device.

The amount of time I have to do that was dramatically reduced when I discovered the Mophie Helium charging case (see Figure 10.6). It is a hard case that you put your phone in. It provides backup power when your phone's battery gets low. The battery pack in the case is charged using a micro-USB port. One feature I particularly like is that you decide when to turn on the backup power and when to turn it off. With judicious use you can actually replenish your phone's battery several times during the day. If you are like me, you want to protect your phone. Although generally I am not careless with my phone, accidents are unavoidable, and when they happen you really hope that it isn't your phone that suffers. I have always put my phones into a case of some kind. A case that also doubles the life of my phone's battery was just too good to miss. I can happily use my phone all day at a conference and not go near an outlet. I'm a heavy phone user, including checking email frequently, updating social networks, and taking pictures. Having the Mophie case has made it possible for me to do all of that and more without worrying about

where my next charge is coming from. Mophie make cases for the most recent
iPhone series (4, 4s, and 5) along with iPods and some Android-based devices.

Figure 10.6   *Mophie Helium charging case (credit Mophie Inc., used with permission)*

If you want to avoid the headache of a diminishing battery charge while you are
on the road, or when you are just away from your desk and don't have access to a
power source, I strongly recommend investing in one of these cases.

Collaboration Tools

One requirement for successful Out of Office working is the ability to collaborate with others. Whether co-workers or clients sharing information, documents,
images, and other work is an essential part of the process. Emailing items back and
forth brings with it the inherent angst of version control. These resources will aid
any team in avoiding those hazards.

Dropbox

I've already mentioned Dropbox in earlier chapters. It is my go-to tool for backing
up my work and for sharing large documents and files with clients and partners.

As you can see from Figure 10.7, Dropbox has a very simple and clean interface:
just a series of files or folders, which at its core is exactly what it is. However, don't
let that simple look fool you. This is a powerful tool, whether used for business

or personal purposes. This figure shows a part of my Dropbox. You can see that the majority of my folders are marked "shared folder." This is how I use Dropbox on a regular basis, as a collaboration tool. Setting up folders to share is extremely straightforward, and if you have ever created a folder on either a PC or Mac, you will already be familiar with the way Dropbox works. Adding files to folders operates in exactly the same way.

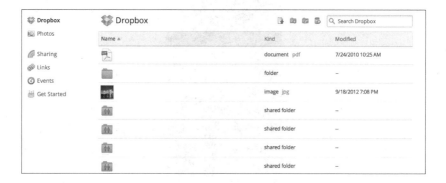

Figure 10.7   *Dropbox (credit Author)*

Folders can be shared with one person or many people, and you can import your contact list to Dropbox to make the process even easier. When you are sharing a folder, you can also decide whether the recipient can share the folder with their contacts.

As a backup tool, Dropbox operates in exactly the same way: Simply save files or copy them to the appropriate folders and they are stored in the cloud.

Dropbox has effectively removed the barrier to moving large files between users. No more restrictions because of an inbox being full or a service provider having limits on the size of files that can be transmitted via email.

It also works extremely well as a knowledge repository. I use it when working with developers to hold scripts, documentation, and other resources so that all team members have access to them without having to rely on one person having the needed resource on their computer.

In addition, I use Dropbox to back up my images. I have the Dropbox app on my phone so that when I take a picture, it is automatically backed up to Dropbox; likewise, when I upload any images to Facebook, they are also backed up. I really like knowing that I will never lose an image when I take it.

Box

Box, shown in Figure 10.8, is similar in nature to Dropbox. However, although it does have a "personal" account type, it is more geared toward the business environment. It operates in much the same way as Dropbox; however, it extends its basic functionality by integrating with several software offerings from other vendors that are familiar to business users, such as Salesforce, Google Apps, Netsuite, and Jive. In addition, Box provides an application programming interface (API) to allow integration with custom-developed software (this feature is also available with Dropbox).

Figure 10.8   *Box (credit Box, used with permission)*

Additional features that make this tool suited to distributed teams is the "Online Workspace." This feature allows users to view, edit, and upload files to a shared folder. Box also offers version tracking, to ensure that users know which version of a document is the most current and which are historical versions. Incorporated into the tool is a basic workflow for documents. This allows a document to be assigned to various users for review, editing, and so on, by a certain date.

With its integration into popular tools such as Microsoft Office and Google Docs, Box positions itself as business friendly and business ready. It boasts an impressive array of corporate users and is definitely a system worth considering when you have a team composed of Out of Office and in-office workers or a fully distributed team.

iDoneThis

Unlike the other systems mentioned in this section, iDoneThis (shown in Figure 10.9) has no storage capability, nor does it have cool online editing tools or version control. What it does do is the one aspect of remote team management that most people dislike: It manages updates on project progress.

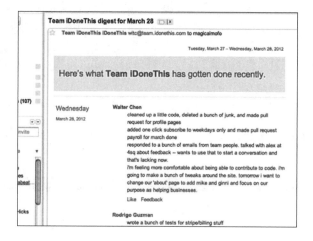

Figure 10.9   *iDoneThis (credit iDoneThis, used with permission)*

The system sends an email to each member of the team at the end of the workday that simply asks, "What did you get done today?" Each user then replies to the email with a summary of what they accomplished.

The following morning the system aggregates the replies and sends a digest out to everyone. What I like about this concept is that it allows a team to stay in touch, keep track of progress, and to do so without a complicated system. In addition, using filters or just simple file management, a record can be kept of the progress each team member has made with various projects. I see this type of system being a way to cut down on basic "update" meetings and freeing up time for team members to get more work done. One additional use I see for this type of tool is allowing managers to keep ongoing notes for use in performance reviews. One task I know that many managers find hard to complete on an annual or semi-annual basis is performance reviews. This problem can become compounded with Out of Office employees who are not such a physical presence. Using this type of system allows managers to keep a record of achievements over a period of time.

Microsoft SkyDrive

Similar to Dropbox and Box, this cloud storage service from Microsoft is geared toward Microsoft users. It integrates with Microsoft Office and Hotmail, along with Microsoft 360, the online version of Microsoft Office. The name of the product is going to change shortly after a legal dispute with BSkyB, a satellite television company in the UK. No information on what the new name will be was available at the time of writing.

iCloud

Primarily a cloud storage service for Apple users, iCloud offers integration with Apple devices. It allows images, music, and other media to be downloaded on one device and be accessible from other Apple devices that share the same iCloud account.

Like Microsoft's SkyDrive, it is geared toward an existing user base. Although it does support document storage and editing, it only does this for Apple's proprietary software iWork.

If you (or your organization) are using Apple products exclusively, then this is a good option as because comes preinstalled on all new Mac and iOS-based products.

Productivity Assistants

As much as we might like to think of ourselves as dedicated, task-oriented production machines (OK, I'm not actually sure I know anyone who seriously thinks of themselves that way outside of an annual review), we all have moments where we find the internet or other distractions just a little too fascinating, to the point where they actually impede our productivity. These tools might just help you stay on track.

RescueTime

We've all done it: You go online to research something for your job and somehow find yourself chasing links down a rabbit-hole, or you find yourself on a social media site looking at photos of your friend's kittens.

RescueTime allows you to control the amount of time you spend on certain sites by blocking them for a while. Although this seems a little like "parental controls" for adults, I think it helps individuals focus on the task at hand without wandering.

Where RescueTime really comes into its own, though, is as a time-tracking tool. Figure 10.10 shows a chart of how a user has spent their time with various programs on their computer. If you are involved in any type of billable hours fee structure (for example, as a freelancer), this is a valuable tool to show you how to bill clients for work you have performed.

Figure 10.10   *RescueTime (credit RescueTime, used with permission)*

In addition, as RescueTime cites, if you want to know how many licenses your company actually needs for a piece of software, take a look at how many people across the organization actually use it—not only a time saver but a cost saver as well. Of course, some employees might find it a little "Orwellian" to have their computer use monitored and assessed, but that is a whole different discussion about organizational culture.

Overall, I think tools such as RescueTime are more of a benefit than a hindrance, and the ability to get tangible data on how you spend your time on the computer is another way to achieve the integration lifestyle I refer to in Chapter 8, "Work/Life Integration." If you are only guessing about your activity, then you aren't really enabling yourself to make good decisions.

Coffee Break

Taking a break from what you are working on can actually improve productivity. That sounds counterintuitive, but regular breaks away from a computer help reset your eyes (thus avoiding eyestrain) and enable you to stretch (thus avoiding lower back problems and a whole host of other physical issues). This also allows you to collect your thoughts.

Coffee Break (currently only available on Mac) allows you to set multiple breaks throughout the day, determine how long those breaks should be, whether they should darken your screen, and how dark and various other elements that give you a reason to step away from the computer (see Figure 10.11).

Figure 10.11   *Coffee Break (credit iLifeTouch, used with permission)*

Again, these tools have a "parental" feel to them, but if you are like me, it is all too easy to become so focused that an entire day can slip by without you having taken a break. I have often found myself eating lunch at 4 p.m., which of course throws off my appetite for dinner—which is fine if you are the only one in the house, but when you have a partner, not being hungry at dinnertime can become a friction point if you aren't careful.

Regular breaks also mean that you are taking care of yourself, something that Out of Office workers are prone not to do. Being aware of the need for breaks, ensuring that your routine includes exercise and healthy eating, and taking care of your mental health are all part of the investment that you need to make in yourself when you decide to work Out of Office. Coffee Break is available at the Mac App Store.

Breaker

Like Coffee Break, Breaker helps you enforce regular breaks away from your computer. Breaker is currently only available on PC. Where it differs from Coffee Break
is that it not only reminds you to take a break, but can also be used to remind you
to go back to work (see Figure 10.12).

Figure 10.12 *Breaker (credit Breaker, used with permission)*

With a timer feature similar to RescueTime, Breaker can log how much time you
have spent working in any given period. If you are working on a single project and
running Breaker, this can be an effective way of measuring your billable time. In
addition to the time-tracking feature, you can also have Breaker remind you it is
time to go back to work. I like this idea. Although being reminded it is time to take
a break is important, it is just as important to ensure that those ten-minute coffee
breaks don't stretch to 60 minutes.

Breaker doesn't have the most attractive user interface, but it does what it is meant
to do, so I guess looking attractive isn't as essential. Breaker can be found at http://
davidevitelaru.com/software/breaker/.

There is a downside to these types of tools: Some people find that they increase
their stress levels. The reminders to take a break interfere with the workflow that
the users have established, and the way that these timers operate can become a
point of stress. I can see how they might become like an annoying work colleague
who constantly drops by your office or cube and asks you if you want to take a
break or whether it is time for lunch yet.

Whether you allow these reminders to become a point of stress is up to you. I personally think having a reminder set to take a break every now and then is another good way to achieve integration. My suggestion would be to find your own rhythm before implementing one of these timers, see where the breaks occur naturally, and then set reminders for them.

Index

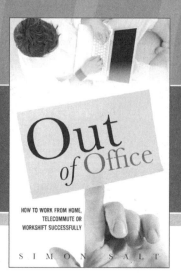

Safari
Books Online

FREE
Online Edition

Your purchase of **Out of Office** includes access to a free online edition for 45 days through the **Safari Books Online** subscription service. Nearly every Que book is available online through **Safari Books Online**, along with thousands of books and videos from publishers such as Addison-Wesley Professional, Cisco Press, Exam Cram, IBM Press, O'Reilly Media, Prentice Hall, and Sams.

Safari Books Online is a digital library providing searchable, on-demand access to thousands of technology, digital media, and professional development books and videos from leading publishers. With one monthly or yearly subscription price, you get unlimited access to learning tools and information on topics including mobile app and software development, tips and tricks on using your favorite gadgets, networking, project management, graphic design, and much more.

Activate your FREE Online Edition at
informit.com/safarifree

STEP 1:   Enter the coupon code: GMPZQZG.

STEP 2:   New Safari users, complete the brief registration form.
Safari subscribers, just log in.

If you have difficulty registering on Safari or accessing the online edition,
please e-mail customer-service@safaribooksonline.com

Addison Wesley   AdobePress   ALPHA   Cisco Press   FT Press   IBM Press   Microsoft Press   New Riders   O'REILLY

Peachpit Press   PRENTICE HALL   QUE   Redbooks   SAMS   SAS Publishing   vmware PRESS   WILEY   wrox